D0547606

OAT CUISINE

OAT CUISINE

The New Oat Recipe Cookbook

foulsham

LONDON • NEW YORK • TORONTO • SYDNEY

foulsham

The Publishing House, Bennetts Close, Cippenham,
Slough, Berkshire SL1 5AP, England

ISBN 0–572–02660–9

Printed in Malaysia

CONTENTS

INTRODUCTION

In the last few years, so much has been written about what we should and should not eat that it is easy to be sceptical about the latest dietary advice. Oats have been around for centuries, and a bowl of porridge has always been considered a satisfying breakfast.

We now know that there are two types of dietary fibre: insoluble and soluble. Bran is insoluble and, although valuable in its own way, it should be eaten with foods that contain soluble fibre. Which is where oats come in because they (as well as beans) are the best sources of soluble fibre, a type of fibre that scientific research has shown can help maintain a healthy heart as part of a low-fat diet.

Oats are a wonderfully versatile cooking ingredient. Traditional porridge and muesli are simple and obvious ways to include oats in your diet, but you'll also find plenty of innovative recipes here for using them in main meals, desserts and delicious bakes.

MILLING OATS SINCE 1675

Not many companies today can trace their history back to 325 years before the current millennium began, but Mornflake can, having first milled oats in the beautiful Cheshire countryside for local farmers in 1675!

Today, 14 generations later, the company is still independently owned and managed by the direct descendants of those millers. With expertise and skills handed down from fathers to sons, this unparalleled experience ensures that you can continue to enjoy oat products of the highest possible quality from Mornflake.

No wonder Mornflake oats regularly win the European milling industry's top International Gold Medals for quality, purity and consistency. The way Mornflake mill oats carefully retains the whole grain containing both germ and bran, removing only the inedible outer husk. Modern technology at this 'state-of-the-art' mill is so sophisticated that the grain can be precisely sorted for shape, size and moisture so it is optimised for each of the many types of oat product, from rolled oats to oatmeals and oat flours.

IMPROVING YOUR DIET

IMPROVING YOUR DIET
We could all do with making a few changes to our lifestyle and our diet. To include more soluble fibre is one of those changes that would benefit us all.

ARE YOU AT RISK?
A number of factors may affect our lifestyle in terms of diet. Some you can change, others you can't. They include:

Family history

Age

Smoking

Alcohol

Overweight

Lack of exercise

Stress

High levels of LDL cholesterol

If any of these factors plays a part in your lifestyle, it makes sense to act to change the situation. Aiming for a healthy, balanced diet is one important change you can make and this chapter will give you some guidelines on planning that healthy diet. Your diet should be made up primarily of unrefined carbohydrates together with protein and a small amount of fat. If you focus on fresh rather than processed foods, you will also have all the essential vitamins and minerals the body needs. And if you are following a sensible diet, the occasional high-fat or high-sugar treats will do you no harm at all!

EAT MORE FIBRE AND WHOLE FOODS
We should make sure that our diet is made up of foods which are high in fibre, particularly soluble fibre. Eat plenty of pasta, wholemeal bread and potatoes; they are not fattening or bad for us – that is now a myth consigned to gather dust by today's nutritionists (as long as you don't smother them with butter or rich sauces). Include lots of cereals, like oats, fruit and vegetables. These foods are also rich in the protective antioxidant vitamins.

Sprinkling bran on everything you eat or relying on a bran breakfast cereal as many people do is not the best way to increase the amount of fibre in your diet. Too much raw bran can bind minerals, making them unavailable to the body. Bran cures constipation, but does not share the cholesterol-lowering effects of foods containing soluble fibre.

Most of us eat less than half the fibre we need. According to health experts we should be eating 25–35 g/1–1½ oz of fibre every day. At least 7 g/¼ oz of this should be soluble fibre.

Easy ways to boost your fibre intake
- Eat more oats, bread, pasta, rice and potatoes. Choose wholemeal varieties when possible.
- Add pulses (beans, peas and lentils) and whole grains like barley, millet and bulgar to your cooking. Try using them to replace some of the meat in dishes such as spaghetti bolognaise and shepherd's pie.
- Breakfast cereals are good for you. If you don't fancy porridge every morning, choose other wholegrain cereals with little or no added sugar.
- Eat at least five portions of fruit and vegetables every day. Wash fruit like apples but leave them unpeeled, and eat the skins of new and jacket potatoes. Enjoy dried fruit such as prunes, dates, figs, apricots and peaches.

This process in itself will mean that you are eating more fresh foods and fewer refined foods in your diet and you will therefore have the benefit of all the natural vitamins and minerals from the foods.

CUT DOWN ON FAT
Aim for less than 75 g/3 oz of fat a day, including the invisible fats in cakes and pastries, and cooking oils. This means not eating too many pastries, pies or crisps. Use polyunsaturated vegetable oil and spreads instead of saturated fats (butter, hard margarine and lard). Don't add fat when cooking; roasting is very successful without extra fat and you can cook foods in foil to allow them to cook in their own natural juices. Grill rather than fry; and if you do fry foods occasionally, use a heavy-based non-stick pan with little or no added fat. Make use of herbs and spices to add flavour to food, rather than fat, and add oatmeal to soups, sauces and casseroles as a thickener instead of fat or flour.

Choose lean cuts of meat and eat meat in moderation. Swap at least one meat meal a week for fish; cod, haddock and other white fish are low in fat. Oily fish, such as salmon, mackerel and sardines, are an excellent source of omega 3 fatty acids. These help to reduce blood viscosity, making it less likely to clot and therefore cause obstructions in the arteries.

Make low-fat substitutes wherever possible: skimmed or semi-skimmed for full-fat milk, lower-fat cheeses such as Mozzarella or Brie, and so on.

Remember, though, that some lower-fat alternatives may still contain a substantial amount of fat.

CUT DOWN ON SUGAR

Sugar does not supply any nutritional needs; it is just 'empty' calories, and we get all the energy we need from unrefined carbohydrate foods, so keep sugar to a minimum by not adding it to drinks or sprinkling it on cereals, and by cutting down on cakes and biscuits. If you are eating more whole foods, you will already have reduced your intake of processed foods, but remember that sugar – and also salt – are often 'hidden' in processed foods, so read the labels and remember that glucose, syrups, dextrose, etc. are all types of sugar.

A word on alcohol here. Alcohol is also 'empty' calories and, in addition, robs the body of nutrients in order to digest it. However, research has shown that a moderate intake of alcohol can have health benefits so, as in all things, the key is moderation.

CUT DOWN ON SALT

Make a start by not sprinkling salt on food at the table and cutting down the amount you use in cooking – it is possible to wean yourself off salt and rediscover the real taste of food. Use fresh herbs for more flavour. Watch out for hidden salt in processed foods by reading the labels.

STOP SMOKING AND START EXERCISING

Although diet is crucial, if you eat the best diet in the world but continue to smoke, you are risking your health. It is not always easy to stop, but the most important factor is wanting to stop, so investigate ways which will be successful for you.

Most of us need to exercise more, but how much is enough? A 20-minute session of aerobic exercise – brisk walking, cycling or swimming, for example – three times a week is the ideal. However, new research has shown that even moderate and less intense exercise is beneficial – even half an hour once a week is better than just thinking about it! Exercise also helps keep the muscles – and you – in shape, which is just as important as watching the weight on the scales.

MENU IDEAS

Breakfast dishes
- Porridge
- Muesli or granola cereal with oats and dried fruits
- Oat or wholemeal muffins, pancakes, waffles or scones

- Wholemeal bread, scones or rolls thinly spread with polyunsaturated margarine and no-added-sugar preserves or yeast extract
- Fresh or dried fruits
- Natural yoghurt
- Free-range eggs
- Brown rice kedgeree
- Mushrooms cooked in stock and served on toast

Drinks
- Mineral water
- Skimmed or semi-skimmed milk
- Fresh fruit juices
- Herb teas or decaffeinated coffee

Lunch or dinner dishes
- Vegetable, pulse or pasta soups
- Grilled or poached fish, poultry or game
- Quiches or pies with wholemeal or oat pastry
- Vegetable crumbles topped with wholemeal flour, cheese and oats
- Pulse dishes such as chilli con carne, salads or casseroles
- Brown rice dishes such as paella, risotto, curry, stuffed vegetables, kedgeree or salads
- Wholemeal or buckwheat pasta or pizza
- Fish- or vegetable-stuffed wholemeal or oat pancakes
- Poultry with oat stuffing for extra fibre
- Wholemeal or oat bread sandwiches, scones or pitta breads filled with salad and beans
- Salads with fresh vegetables, fruit, beans or nuts, rice or pasta
- Vegetable-based burgers
- Muesli – it's an anytime meal!

Desserts
- Natural yoghurt – on its own or with fresh fruit or honey
- Fresh fruit salads and platters
- Fruit-based crumbles with wholemeal and/or oat crumble topping
- Pancakes with fruit fillings or lemon and honey toppings
- Ice-cream topped with toasted Mornflake oatmeal
- Fools made with fresh or dried fruits with crunchy oat topping
- Low-fat cheesecakes with crunchy oat biscuit bases
- Fruit tarts with wholemeal and oat pastry bases

WHERE DO OATS COME FROM?

You might think that breakfast cereals were a product of the late twentieth century. Not true! Archaeologists have found evidence that the Ancient Greeks and Romans enjoyed tucking into a bowl of porridge. Because oats are a hardy crop, able to survive extreme cold, oats were eaten by tribes throughout northern Europe. When oats reached Scotland they were known as 'pilcorn' and soon became part of the daily fare. Today they remain as popular as ever and David Henderson from Montrose in Scotland – who died in 1998 at the age of 109 and is the longest-living Briton on record – attributed his age and good health to hard work and a daily bowl of porridge.

Throughout the Middle Ages, oatmeal cakes and cheese were the monotonous staple of the British peasant's diet. In the seventeenth and eighteenth century, oats gradually replaced barley and rye because they grew better, but eventually the rapid developments in agriculture resulted in a decline in oat production as they were replaced by wheat.

The revival of oats came with the famous American doctor, John Kellogg. Although he is best known for inventing Cornflakes in 1899, he also created 'granola', an oat-based cereal, in the 1860s. Together with Shredded Wheat and Weetabix – the only cereal invented in England – these cereals were sold as health foods. At the beginning of the nineteenth century, a Swiss nutritionist, Dr Bircher, adapted the old Swiss custom of mixing porridge oats with fresh or dried fruit to create muesli (a German word meaning 'mixture'). He gave it to patients at his health clinic in Zurich and it soon became popular all over Europe, Gradually oats became fashionable again.

Today oats are grown in almost every part of the world but the most important areas of production are North America, Scandinavia, Russia, Great Britain and Australia.

TYPES OF OATS

Oats are an extremely versatile cereal and are available from Mornflake in many grades for breakfasts and cooking.

Rolled or flaked oats

These are given many different names but are basically the same type of product. Mornflake produce them under the name Superfast Oats; flaked oats, oat flakes, quick oats, rolled oats, easy oats and porridge oats are some of the common names also used. They are partially cooked during the milling process and are ideal for making porridge, muesli, parkin and flapjack biscuits.

Jumbo oats

These are the largest variety of flaked oat and are ideal for making a good, thick porridge with a more pronounced texture. They have a slightly nutty flavour and make superb biscuits and an excellent base for muesli.

Mornflake organic oats

Organic oats are made from oats specially grown to the established organic standards laid down by the UK Register of Organic Food Standards, by which the crops rely for their purity on the goodness of the soil, enriched only by natural means.

Every oat crop under contract for Mornflake Organic Oats is grown to strict standards by farmers who use traditional farming methods without any chemical fertilisers.

Oatmeal

Medium oatmeal is made from ground whole-grain oats and has a pleasant, slightly rough texture, ideal for porridge, oatcakes and parkin. Medium oatmeal is the best variety for coating fish and meat before frying and is good in stuffings and crumble toppings.

Fine oatmeal makes a lovely, smooth milk pudding. This is the type to use as a thickening agent for soups, sauces and gravy.

Coarse oatmeal is, as its name suggests, similar to medium oatmeal but is ground to a coarser grade for extra texture.

Pinhead oatmeal can be made into delicious traditional Scottish porage, which is more granular than the porridge most people are used to. Pinhead oatmeal is the chunkiest grade of oatmeal in general usage and can be ideal for adding texture as well as nutritional value to soups, stews and toppings for pies and puddings.

Oat bran

Oat bran is milled from the two thin layers which are found beneath the outer husk or 'hull' of the oat grain. These layers are particularly rich in soluble fibre. Oat bran makes a very smooth porridge and can be sprinkled into many recipes, including cereals and salad dishes, or used in baking for higher-fibre food.

Oat flour

Oat flour is very fine, smooth-textured flour. Ideal as a baby food, it also makes a good thickening agent. Mixed with wheat flour, it is delicious in biscuits, bread, cakes, scones and pastry.

Making oat flour

Oat flour is not as readily available in supermarkets as other products, but it is easy to make your own. Simply place some Mornflake oats or fine or medium Mornflake oatmeal in a liquidiser or food processor and grind to flour. Keep a jar ready made up to add oat power to your cooking!

HOW WE MAKE MORNFLAKE OATS

When oats arrive at the mill they contain all sorts of impurities – ranging from seeds to much larger substances, like iron, coal, straw, sticks and stones! – which all have to be removed. The oats are then dried, conditioned and stored in bins until required.

The miller has to obtain from the oat the kernel from which oatmeal and porridge oats are made and, to do this, a variety of machines and different processes are used.

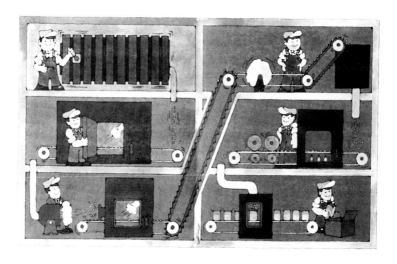

1 Cleaning

All the extraneous matter has to be removed from the grain while it is still in its whole state. This is accomplished by the use of many ingenious machines which take advantage of the differences in size, shape, specific gravity and colour of the grain and the impurities. This is done by sieves, currents of air, which we call aspirators, and by indented cylinders or discs which pick up the smaller grain or seeds and leave the larger grain, which passes on to the next stage.

2 Roasting or kilning

The oat passes through a machine which blows hot air from a furnace over it and dries the grain down from its natural moisture content of 16 per cent to approximately 6 per cent. It is then cooled and stored (or conditioned, as we all it), until it is required for the next process.

3 Shelling or removal of husk

The oats are shelled by passing through a machine which throws the oat at a very high speed against a stationary rubber surface. This has the effect of springing the kernel, or groat, from the shell before the whole mass passes over an aspirator, which is able to blow away the oat husk because of its lighter density. This enables the miller to separate the husk and to grind it directly into cattle feed, while the groat passes on to the next stage.

4 Polishing, cutting, grading and cleaning

The groat now passes through polishers and over a table separator which extracts any unshelled oats and returns them to the shelling process. The groat is cut on rotary granulators, each groat being cut into three pieces. It is then graded on rotary sieves and aspirated to blow away any small pieces of oat husk. From this point the meal is called pinhead oatmeal, and this is then stored until it is required for cooking into porridge oats.

5 Cooking, flaking and drying

The pinhead oatmeal is passed over a cooker where it is cooked with high-temperature steam. This has the effect of reducing the time required for cooking when porridge is made. After cooking, the pinhead oatmeal is flaked on a flaking roll and it is then dried on a drying band, cooled and packed.

6 Packing

Automatic packing machines are used to pack Mornflake oats into cartons and visi-pillow packs. Machines fill these packs by weight, and these are then placed into corrugated fibreboard cases for delivery to the shops ready for you to enjoy.

YOUR OWN PERSONAL HEALTH FARM

Taking a few days out at a health farm or health hydro is an expensive business but it is possible, with a little will-power, to get the same benefits at home. You may not receive the same degree of pampering, true, but if you follow the short health break outlined here, you are sure to enjoy a relaxing and beneficial few days.

Firstly, set aside two or three days when you have no other distractions or commitments. You may need to ask your parents to take the children away for the weekend. You may want to spend time with your partner or on your own. Perhaps you would like to ask a friend to come over and join you. Then read through the diet so that you can do all your shopping in advance and plan how you are going to fill those wonderful, relaxing hours with things that you really enjoy!

FRIDAY'S MEALS

At work, avoid your regular tea and coffee and instead drink mineral water and/or fruit and vegetable juices. Skip the Friday lunchtime visit to the pub and have a wholemeal sandwich or salad for lunch.

When you get home you can relax and start the healthy break with a nutritious mixed salad as your evening meal. Make up your salad from any of the following, choosing a mixture of leaves and roots: watercress, mustard and cress, sweetcorn, beetroot (raw and grated or cooked), tomato, carrots, celery, red or green peppers, courgettes, parsley, lettuce, white or red cabbage, baby turnips or parsnips, grated or shredded spinach, apples, sultanas, raisins, fennel.

Add to the salad: unsalted nuts, sunflower or pumpkin seeds, cooked whole wheat berries or brown rice, chick peas, beans or other pulses. Dress the salad with a little olive oil, freshly pressed lemon or orange juice and a pinch of ready-made wholegrain mustard. Eat some wholemeal bread with the salad if you wish.

Always remember to take your time over your meals throughout the weekend, chew well and relax afterwards.

To drink over the weekend, choose from mineral water (still or sparkling), fruit and/or vegetable juices and herb teas. If you cannot go without coffee, use decaffeinated, but keep it to a minimum.

SATURDAY'S MEALS

Start the day with home-made muesli. To make your muesli, mix together Mornflake oats, millet flakes, flaked almonds or chopped hazelnuts, raisins or sultanas, sunflower or pumpkin seeds. Cover with juice, water or natural yoghurt and leave to soak overnight. Top with natural yoghurt or fresh fruit in the morning, or grate in a small, unpeeled eating apple.

For lunch, serve a large salad, made from any of the ingredients outlined in Friday's section, together with wholemeal, rye or granary bread.

The evening meal on Saturday is a brown rice risotto made with a mixture of root and leaf vegetables. Lightly sauté the diced or shredded vegetables in a little corn or soy oil, stir in the rice, then pour over boiling vegetable stock and leave the mixture to simmer for 35 minutes until the rice is cooked.

Desserts and snacks throughout Saturday and Sunday should be fresh fruit. You might prefer cleansing fruits like grapes and pears rather than higher-calorie bananas.

SUNDAY

For Sunday breakfast, you could have muesli or you might prefer a lighter breakfast of fresh fruit and natural, unsweetened yoghurt. Alternatively, a dried fruit compôte, made from simmered prunes, dried apricots, dried apple rings, dried peaches and pears is very good, especially if simmered in water with some cloves or cinnamon. Serve it with a little unsweetened natural yoghurt.

For Sunday lunch, prepare a jacket potato and fill it with cottage cheese or low-fat quark flavoured with some freshly cut herbs.

Sunday's evening meal is a bean salad made by boiling 50 g/2oz of each of three beans of your choice, such as borlotti, red or black kidney beans, flageolet, haricot or butter beans, then tossing the cooled, cooked beans in salad dressing (see Friday) and mixing with grated carrots, cabbage and celery, apple and a little cooked wholemeal pasta.

EXERCISE

The most important thing about exercise is that you should enjoy it, so choose something you like doing: a game of tennis, a bicycle ride, an aerobic work-out, a yoga class or a run. If you are not the sporty type, go for a long, brisk walk on both days in the park or the countryside. It is rare for the weather to be so bad that you cannot go outdoors, but if that is the case, you can always go for a swim.

RELAXATION

The essential point here is that you switch off from all those stresses of your normal working life. Don't use the time to catch up on office work, clean the house or plan the children's lunch boxes. Read that book you have been meaning to read for months. Do some knitting or craft work. Listen to music. Watch a good video. Enjoy an uninterrupted conversation. Slow down the pace of your life.

If you practise meditation, this will also enhance the benefits of the weekend. If you have never tried it, why not make this the weekend when you actually play that meditation or relaxation-technique cassette you bought months ago!

SOLUBLE FIBRE TABLE

Figures represent grams per 100 grams	Soluble	Insoluble	Total dietary fibre	Energy kCal
Oat-based cereals (sources of beta glucan)				
Mornflake Superfast Oats	3.6	3.6	7.2	364
Mornflake Jumbo Oats	3.6	3.6	7.2	364
Mornflake Oatmeals	3.6	3.6	7.2	364
Mornflake Organic Oats	3.6	3.6	7.2	364
Mornflake Oat Bran	7.3	7.3	14.6	348
Mornflake Hawaiian Crunch	2.6	3.0	5.6	414
Other cereals				
Mornflake Farmhouse Wheatbran	3.3	33.1	36.4	213
All Bran	3.7	18.7	22.4	273
Kellogg's Cornflakes	0.2	0.5	0.7	364
Shredded Wheat	2.1	7.7	9.8	324
Rice Krispies	0.2	0.7	0.9	372
Weetabix	3.1	6.7	9.8	340
Flour and bread				
Cornflour	0.1	0.0	0.1	354
Brown flour	1.9	5.1	7.0	327
Semolina	1.0	1.2	2.3	350
Rye flour	4.0	7.9	11.9	335
White flour	1.4	0.9	2.3	337
Brown bread	1.4	2.9	4.3	223
White bread	1.2	0.4	1.6	233
Rice and pasta				
Macaroni	1.4	1.2	2.6	370
Spaghetti	1.7	1.1	2.8	370
Spaghetti (wholewheat)	2.2	6.8	9.0	338
Brown rice	0.1	1.6	1.7	350
White rice	0.1	0.4	0.5	360
Vegetables and pulses				
Baked beans	1.7	1.5	3.2	64
Brussels sprouts	0.8	2.5	3.3	26
Cabbage	1.3	1.4	2.7	22
Carrots	1.1	1.2	2.3	23
Haricot beans	6.4	8.8	15.2	271
Cooked kidney beans	2.8	3.3	6.1	272
Lettuce	0.4	0.6	1.0	12
Runner beans	0.7	3.7	4.4	26
Potatoes	0.7	0.6	1.3	87
Tomatoes	0.7	1.3	2.0	14
Fruits and nuts				
Apples	0.7	1.2	1.9	46
Bananas	0.6	0.5	1.1	79
Hazelnuts	1.5	2.9	4.4	380
Peanuts	0.9	5.1	6.0	570
Raisins	0.7	1.0	1.7	246

Table compiled by the Oats Health Institute

BREAKFASTS

corn muffins

Makes 12   0.5 g fibre/75 calories each

	METRIC	IMPERIAL	AMERICAN
Free-range egg, separated	1	1	1
Free-range egg yolk	1	1	1
Corn oil	30 ml	2 tbsp	2 tbsp
Milk	30 ml	2 tbsp	2 tbsp
Corn or maize meal	100 g	4 oz	1 cup
Oat flour	50 g	2 oz	½ cup
Baking powder	5 ml	1 tsp	1 tsp
No-added-sugar jam, to serve			

1 Preheat the oven to 200°C/400°F/gas mark 6 and lightly oil a muffin tin.

2 Beat together the egg yolks, oil and milk. Whisk the egg white until stiff.

3 Mix the corn or maize meal, oat flour and baking powder in a bowl. Mix in the liquid, fold in the egg white and spoon the mixture into the prepared muffin tin.

4 Bake in the oven for 20 minutes until risen and golden. Remove from the oven and leave to cool slightly before removing from the tin and serving warm. Delicious for breakfast with no-added-sugar jam.

Cook's note

Remember you can make your own oat flour by grinding some Mornflake oats or oatmeal in a food processor (see page 16).

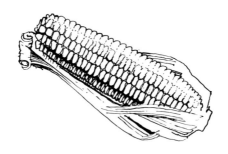

dr anderson's oat muffins

Makes 24   2 g fibre/63 calories per muffin

	METRIC	IMPERIAL	AMERICAN
Mornflake oat bran	100 g	4 oz	2 cups
Oat flour	100 g	4 oz	1 cup
Wholemeal flour	225 g	8 oz	2 cups
Baking powder	10 ml	2 tsp	2 tsp
Skimmed milk	350 ml	12 fl oz	1⅓ cups
Vegetable oil	10 ml	2 tsp	2 tsp
Egg whites	2	2	2

Variations
Add either 50 g/2 oz/⅓ cup of raisins, or 150 ml/¼ pt/⅔ cup of apple purée, or 1 diced pear.

1   Preheat the oven to 190°C/375°F/gas mark 5 and lightly oil a muffin tin.

2   Mix the oat bran, flours and baking powder in a bowl. Stir in the raisins, if using.

3   Mix together the milk and oil and add to the flour with the apple purée, raisins or diced pear, if using.

4   Whisk the egg whites until stiff, then fold into the mixture.

5   Spoon into the muffin tin and bake in the oven for about 25 minutes until risen and golden.

fig muffins

Makes 8   2 g fibre/118 calories per muffin

	METRIC	IMPERIAL	AMERICAN
Sesame or sunflower oil	45 ml	3 tbsp	3 tbsp
Skimmed milk	75 ml	5 tbsp	5 tbsp
Black treacle	15 ml	1 tbsp	1 tbsp
Wholemeal flour	100 g	4 oz	1 cup
Baking powder	5 ml	1 tsp	1 tsp
Mornflake oats	50 g	2 oz	½ cup
Dried figs, finely chopped	50 g	2 oz	⅓ cup
Free-range egg, lightly beaten	1	1	1

1 Preheat the oven to 190°C/375°F/gas mark 5 and lightly oil a muffin tin.

2 Melt the oil, 45 ml/3 tbsp of the milk and the black treacle in a saucepan over a low heat or in the microwave. Remove from the heat.

3 Mix the flour, baking powder, oats and figs. Pour in the oil mixture, then the egg and the remaining milk.

4 Spoon the mixture into the tin and bake in the oven for 20–25 minutes until firm and golden brown.

family favourite granola

Makes 14 servings   3 g fibre/190 calories per serving

	METRIC	IMPERIAL	AMERICAN
Sesame, corn or soya oil	60 ml	4 tbsp	4 tbsp
Clear honey	30 ml	2 tbsp	2 tbsp
Vanilla essence	3 drops	3 drops	3 drops
Mornflake oats	100 g	4 oz	1 cup
Mornflake jumbo oats	100 g	4 oz	1 cup
Sunflower seeds	50 g	2 oz	½ cup
Hazelnuts, half whole/ half chopped	50 g	2 oz	½ cup
Flaked almonds	50 g	2 oz	½ cup
Desiccated coconut	50 g	2 oz	½ cup
Mornflake Farmhouse Wheatbran	50 g	2 oz	1 cup
Raisins or sultanas	50 g	2 oz	⅓ cup

1 Preheat the oven to 190°C/375°F/gas mark 5 and lightly oil a large shallow baking tin.

2 Melt the oil and honey over a low heat. Remove from heat and add the vanilla essence.

3 Place all the remaining ingredients except the raisins or sultanas in a bowl and stir in the oil and honey.

4 Spoon into the prepared tin and bake in the oven for 30 minutes, stirring and turning the mixture every 5–7 minutes to ensure it is evenly toasted. Remove from oven and leave to cool.

5 Stir in the raisins or sultanas and leave until completely cold before storing in an airtight container.

fruit and nut muesli

Serves 8   7.7 g fibre/330 calories per portion

	METRIC	IMPERIAL	AMERICAN
Sunflower seeds	75 g	3 oz	¾ cup
Dried apricots, roughly chopped	75 g	3 oz	½ cup
Stoned dates, roughly chopped	75 g	3 oz	½ cup
Almonds, finely chopped	75 g	3 oz	¾ cup
Walnuts, finely chopped	75 g	3 oz	¾ cup
Mornflake oats	225 g	8 oz	2 cups
Mornflake jumbo oats	100 g	4 oz	I cup

1 Toast the sunflower seeds in a dry frying pan, shaking until golden.

2 Mix together all the ingredients and store in an airtight container until required.

hot waffles

Makes 8   1.5 g fibre/135 calories per waffle

	METRIC	IMPERIAL	AMERICAN
Wholemeal flour	100 g	4 oz	1 cup
Oat flour	50 g	2 oz	½ cup
Baking powder	10 ml	2 tsp	2 tsp
Free-range eggs, separated	2	2	2
Skimmed milk	300 ml	½ pt	1¼ cups
Soft vegetable margarine, melted	50 g	2 oz	¼ cup
Natural yoghurt, fresh fruit, fruit purée, stewed fruit or honey, to serve			

1   Mix the flours and baking powder and make a well in the centre.

2   Lightly beat the egg yolks with a little of the milk, then gradually whisk into the flour. Gradually whisk in the remaining milk.

3   Carefully drizzle the melted margarine into the batter. Whisk the egg whites until stiff, then fold them into the mixture.

4   Heat the waffle maker and add 30–45 ml/2–3 tbsp of batter. Close the lid and cook for 1–2 minutes until golden brown. Keep the waffles warm while you cook the remaining batter.

5   Serve hot with accompaniments of your choice.

oatmeal porridge

Serves 2   7 g fibre/100 calories

	METRIC	IMPERIAL	AMERICAN
Mornflake medium oatmeal	30 ml	2 tbsp	2 tbsp
Water	600 ml	1 pt	2¼ cups
Sea salt			

Mix the oatmeal and water in a saucepan, bring to the boil and simmer for a few minutes until the oatmeal is swollen and tender. Season to taste with salt.

coconut muesli

Serves 4   5 g fibre/250 calories per portion

	METRIC	IMPERIAL	AMERICAN
Mornflake oats	60 ml	4 tbsp	4 tbsp
Millet flakes	30 ml	2 tbsp	2 tbsp
Sunflower seeds	15 ml	1 tbsp	1 tbsp
Raisins	15 ml	1 tbsp	1 tbsp
Flaked almonds	15 ml	1 tbsp	1 tbsp
Ground coconut	15 ml	1 tbsp	1 tbsp
Mornflake Farmhouse Wheatbran	15 ml	1 tbsp	1 tbsp
Fruit juice, mineral water, natural yoghurt or buttermilk, to soak			

1 Mix together all the ingredients except the soaking liquid.

2 Place portions of muesli in breakfast bowls and soak overnight in either fruit juice (such as apple juice), mineral water, natural yoghurt or buttermilk.

fruity porridge

Serves 4   4.5 g fibre/240 calories per portion

	METRIC	IMPERIAL	AMERICAN
Mornflake oats	175 g	6 oz	1½ cups
Mornflake Farmhouse Wheatbran	50 g	2 oz	½ cup
Raisins	50 g	2 oz	⅓ cup
Water	300–450 ml	½–¾ pt	1¼–2 cups
Eating apples, cored but not peeled	2	2	2

1 Place the oats, bran and raisins in a saucepan. Add the water, place over a low heat and bring to a simmer, stirring continuously to prevent sticking. The amount of water needed will depend on the absorbency of the oats and the texture you prefer.

2 Grate the apples into the porridge just before serving.

plain porridge

Serves 1   7 g fibre/100 calories

	METRIC	IMPERIAL	AMERICAN
Mornflake oats	30 ml	2 tbsp	2 tbsp
Skimmed milk or water	150 ml	¼ pt	⅔ cup
Sea salt			

1   The proportions of porridge are 1 part oats to 2–2½ parts liquid. If you use jumbo oats, you will need a slightly longer cooking time.

2   Mix the oats and milk or water in a saucepan and bring to the boil. Stir for about 1 minute until thick and creamy. Season to taste with salt.

3   To make porridge in a 650W microwave, mix in a suitable bowl. Cook on Full power for 1½ minutes, stir, then cook for a further ¾–1 minute. Stir and add salt to taste before serving. Reduce the cooking time for higher-powered microwaves.

wheatbran muffins

Makes 12   2 g fibre/140 calories per muffin

	METRIC	IMPERIAL	AMERICAN
Sesame oil	45 ml	3 tbsp	3 tbsp
Clear honey	30 ml	2 tbsp	2 tbsp
Black treacle	15 ml	1 tbsp	1 tbsp
Wholemeal flour	100 g	4 oz	1 cup
Mornflake Farmhouse Wheatbran	50 g	2 oz	½ cup
Mornflake oats	50 g	2 oz	½ cup
Baking powder	15 ml	1 tbsp	1 tbsp
Free-range egg	1	1	1
Sultanas	100 g	4 oz	⅔ cup
Walnuts, chopped	50 g	2 oz	½ cup
Eating apple, grated	1	1	1
Water	90 ml	6 tbsp	6 tbsp

1 Preheat the oven to 190°C/375°F/gas mark 5 and lightly oil a muffin tin.

2 Warm the oil, honey and black treacle in a saucepan.

3 Mix together all the remaining ingredients except the water, then pour on the melted mixture and stir well. Add enough water to give a soft dropping consistency.

4 Spoon the mixture into the tin and bake in the oven for 20–30 minutes until well risen and golden brown.

soft oat muffins

Makes 16 muffins   1 g fibre/70 calories per muffin

	METRIC	IMPERIAL	AMERICAN
Mornflake oats	100 g	4 oz	1 cup
Water	300 ml	½ pt	1¼ cups
Vegetable oil	30 ml	2 tbsp	2 tbsp
Black treacle	15 ml	1 tbsp	1 tbsp
Sultanas	75 g	3 oz	½ cup
Wholemeal flour	50 g	2 oz	½ cup
Baking powder	10 ml	2 tsp	2 tsp
Eating apple, peeled and grated	1	1	1
OR Carrot, grated	1 large	1 large	1 large
Free-range egg, beaten	1	1	1

1   Preheat the oven to 190°C/375°F/gas mark 5 and lightly oil a muffin tin.

2   Place the oats and water in saucepan and bring to the boil, then continue to stir over a low heat until the mixture is the thickness of porridge. Remove from the heat.

3   Place the oil, treacle and sultanas in a saucepan over a low heat and stir gently until melted.

4   Mix the flour and baking powder in a bowl. Add the cooled porridge and stir well. Stir in the treacle mixture and add the grated apple or carrot. Stir in the beaten egg.

5   Spoon into the prepared tin and bake in the oven for about 25 minutes until risen and golden.

rich croissants

Makes 16   2 g fibre/190 calories per croissant

	METRIC	IMPERIAL	AMERICAN
Evaporated milk	175 ml	6 fl oz	¾ cup
Water	120 ml	4 fl oz	½ cup
Clear honey	15 ml	1 tbsp	1 tbsp
Fresh yeast	15 g	½ oz	1 tbsp
25 mg vitamin C tablet, crushed	1	1	1
Wholemeal flour	350 g	12 oz	3 cups
Oat flour	100 g	4 oz	1 cup
Unsalted butter	225 g	8 oz	1 cup
Egg, lightly beaten, to glaze	1	1	1

1 Preheat the oven to 230°C/450°F/gas mark 8 and lightly oil two baking sheets.

2 Warm the evaporated milk, water and honey over a low heat until lukewarm. Remove from the heat, crumble in the yeast and vitamin C tablet and mix well.

3 Mix the flours in a bowl, pour in the milk mixture and mix to a dough. Cover and leave to rest.

4 Shape the butter into a rectangle. Use a floured rolling pin and work on a floured surface. Roll out the dough into a large rectangle and place the butter in the centre. Fold the pastry over the butter, then fold into three. Cover and rest in the fridge for 20 minutes.

5 Place the dough with the folded edge away from you, roll out again, then fold into three. Roll out and fold again. Cover the dough and rest in the fridge for 20 minutes. Repeat twice, refrigerating for 20 minutes between each rolling and folding. Cover and rest again for 15–20 minutes before use.

6 Divide the dough in half and roll each half into a large circle. Cut into 16 segments and roll up each croissant from the outside towards the centre. Bend into a crescent shape and place on the baking sheets. Cover and leave to rise in a warm place until doubled in size.

7 Glaze with lightly beaten egg and bake for 20 minutes until golden.

easy croissants

Makes 12   2 g fibre/185 calories per criossant

	METRIC	IMPERIAL	AMERICAN
Wholemeal flour	225 g	8 oz	2 cups
Oat flour	100 g	4 oz	1 cup
Unsalted butter	175 g	6 oz	¾ cup
Fresh yeast	15 g	½ oz	1 tbsp
25 mg vitamin C tablet, crushed	1	1	1
Clear honey	15 ml	1 tbsp	1 tbsp
Skimmed milk	200 ml	7 fl oz	scant 1 cup

Milk or beaten egg, to glaze

1   Preheat the oven to 230°C/450°F/gas mark 8 and lightly oil a baking sheet.

2   Mix the flours in a bowl, then rub the butter in well but not as finely as when making pastry. Crumble in the yeast and vitamin C tablet and stir in the honey.

3   Heat the milk to 200°C/98°F. Pour on to the flour and beat well to form a dough. Cover and leave to stand for 10 minutes.

4   Knead the dough lightly on a floured surface, then roll into a large circle. Cut into quarters, then cut each quarter into three sections, as though cutting a pizza. Roll each section from the outside towards the centre and bend into a crescent shape. Place on the baking sheet, cover and leave until doubled in size.

5   Glaze with milk or beaten egg and bake in the oven for 15–20 minutes until golden.

Cook's note
Remember you can make your own oat flour by grinding some Mornflake oats or oatmeal in a food processor (see page 16).

breakfast scones

Makes 8   2.5 g fibre/150 calories per scone

	METRIC	IMPERIAL	AMERICAN
Water	150 ml	¼ pt	⅔ cup
No-added-sugar muesli	100 g	4 oz	1 cup
Wholemeal flour	100 g	4 oz	1 cup
Baking powder	10 ml	2 tsp	2 tsp
Unsalted butter	50 g	2 oz	¼ cup
Sultanas	50 g	2 oz	⅓ cup

Milk or beaten egg, to glaze

1 Preheat the oven to 230°C/450°F/gas mark 8 and lightly oil a baking sheet.

2 Pour the water over the muesli and leave to soak for about 30 minutes (or overnight in the fridge) until the grains are swollen.

3 Mix the flour and baking powder in a bowl, then rub in the butter until the mixture resembles breadcrumbs. Stir in the sultanas.

4 Add the soaked muesli and stir to a soft dough. Turn on to a lightly floured surface and knead gently until the dough is smooth and holds its shape.

5 Shape into an 18 cm/7 in round, place on the baking sheet and score the top with a sharp knife into eight sections. Glaze with a little milk or beaten egg and bake in the oven for 20 minutes until golden brown.

MAIN MEALS

onion tart

Serves 4   4.5 g fibre/359 calories per portion

	METRIC	IMPERIAL	AMERICAN
1 Oat Pastry Case, baked blind (see page 43)	1	1	1
Vegetable oil	15 ml	1 tbsp	1 tbsp
Onions, diced	2 large	2 large	2 large
Quark, or similar low-fat soft cheese	100 g	4 oz	1 cup
Natural yoghurt	150 ml	¼ pt	⅔ cup
Free-range eggs	2	2	2
Sea salt and freshly ground black pepper			
A pinch of ground mace			

1 Prepare the Oat Pastry Case.

2 While the pastry case is baking, heat the oil and gently fry the onions for a few minutes until soft.

3 Beat together the quark, yoghurt and eggs and season with salt and pepper.

4 Place the onions on kitchen paper to drain off any excess fat, then turn them into the pastry case. Pour the yoghurt mixture on top and return to the oven for 35 minutes until golden brown and set.

oat pancakes with courgette filling

Serves 4   4 g fibre/230 calories per pancake

	METRIC	IMPERIAL	AMERICAN
For the pancakes:			
Wholemeal flour	50 g	2 oz	½ cup
Oat flour	50 g	2 oz	½ cup
Free-range egg, lightly beaten	I	I	I
Skimmed milk	300 ml	½ pt	I ¼ cups
For the filling:			
Courgette, large	I	I	I
Broccoli spears	2	2	2
Aubergine	I small	I small	I small
Leek	I	I	I
Chinese leaves	4	4	4
Carrots	2	2	2
Vegetable oil	I5 ml	I tbsp	I tbsp
Cashew nuts, chopped	I00 g	4 oz	I cup
Sesame oil	I0 ml	2 tsp	2 tsp
Grated root ginger	5 ml	I tsp	I tsp

Sweet and Sour Sauce (page 59), to serve

I   Mix the flours in a bowl and make a well in the centre. Add the egg and milk and gradually blend to a smooth batter.

2   Lightly oil an I8 cm/7 in heavy-based pan and place over a high heat.

3   Using a small jug, pour in enough batter to thinly coat the bottom of the pan, tipping the pan from side to side. Cook the pancake for about I minute until the underside no longer sticks to the pan, then toss the pancake and cook the second side. Cook the remaining pancakes.

4   To prepare the filling, cut all the vegetables into matchsticks.

5   Heat the oil in a wok or large frying pan and stir-fry the vegetables quickly until just soft but still crisp. Mix in the cashew nuts, sesame oil and ginger.

6   Stuff the pancakes with the vegetable mixture, roll up and serve with Sweet and Sour Sauce.

steamed skirlie
or oatmeal stuffing

Serves 4   2 g fibre/80 calories per serving

	METRIC	IMPERIAL	AMERICAN
Mornflake fine oatmeal	225 g	8 oz	2 cups
Suet	100 g	4 oz	½ cup
Sea salt and freshly ground black pepper			
Onion, finely chopped	1 large	1 large	1 large
Milk	30–45 ml	2–3 tbsp	2–3 tbsp

1 Lightly oil a 600 ml/1 pt/2½ cup pudding basin.

2 Mix together the oatmeal and suet and season with salt and pepper. Stir in the onion and the milk. Spoon into the basin, cover and place in a large saucepan. Pour boiling water around the basin to come half way up the sides of the basin, cover and steam for 1 hour, topping up with boiling water as necessary.

3 Serve with mince or poultry.

spinach soufflé

Serves 4   3 g fibre/140 calories per portion

	METRIC	IMPERIAL	AMERICAN
Soft vegetable margarine	50 g	2 oz	¼ cup
Oat flour	50 g	2 oz	1 cup
Skimmed milk	300 ml	½ pt	1¼ cups
Freshly grated nutmeg			
Freshly ground black pepper			
Gruyère cheese, grated	25 g	1 oz	2 tbsp
Spinach, cooked and chopped, or frozen	175 g	6 oz	1½ cups
Free-range eggs, separated	4	4	4
Green salad, to serve			

1   Preheat the oven to 190°C/375°F/gas mark 5 and lightly oil an 18 cm/ 7 in soufflé dish. Make a collar out of a double layer of greaseproof paper which overlaps at least 2.5 cm/1 in at any joins and is 5 cm/2 in higher than the top of the dish. Tie in place with string.

2   Place the margarine and flour in a saucepan and stir over a low heat until blended. Gradually add the milk and stir to make a thick sauce. Add the nutmeg and black pepper and remove from the heat. Stir in the cheese and the spinach. Lightly beat the egg yolks and stir them into the mixture.

3   Whisk the egg whites until stiff, then fold in 30 ml/2 tbsp to lighten the mixture. Fold in the remainder and quickly pour into the prepared soufflé dish.

4   Cook in the oven for 40 minutes until risen and set. Serve immediately with a lightly tossed green salad.

spinach pancakes

Makes 8   6 g fibre/145 calories per pancake

	METRIC	IMPERIAL	AMERICAN
1 quantity of Oat Pancakes (see page 38)			
For the filling:			
Spinach, cooked and chopped, or frozen	225 g	8 oz	2 cups
Oat flour	15 ml	1 tbsp	1 tbsp
Unsalted butter or soft vegetable margarine	15 ml	1 tbsp	1 tbsp
Freshly grated nutmeg			
Sea salt and freshly ground black pepper			
Mature Cheddar cheese, grated	75 g	3 oz	¾ cup

1   Preheat the oven to 180°C/350°F/gas mark 4 and lightly oil a shallow ovenproof dish.

2   Place the spinach in a colander and press down with a small plate to remove the excess water. Place in a liquidiser with the oat flour and butter or margarine and blend to a purée. Place in a saucepan and stir over a low heat until warm, then gradually stir in the milk to make a thick purée. Season to taste with salt and pepper.

3   Divide the mixture equally between the pancakes, roll them up and arrange in a single layer in the prepared dish. Sprinkle with the cheese and bake in the oven for 20 minutes until hot and the cheese is golden.

spinach roulade

Serves 8   2 g fibre/195 calories per serving

	METRIC	IMPERIAL	AMERICAN
Soft vegetable margarine	75 g	3 oz	⅓ cup
Wholemeal flour	50 g	2 oz	½ cup
Oat flour	50 g	2 oz	½ cup
Skimmed milk	600 ml	1 pt	2½ cups
Free-range eggs, separated	3	3	3
Grated Parmesan cheese	30 ml	2 tbsp	2 tbsp
Frozen spinach, thawed and drained	175 g	6 oz	1½ cups
Shelled prawns	175 g	6 oz	1½ cups
Lemon wedges, to serve			

1   Preheat the oven to 180°C/350°F/gas mark 4 and line a small Swiss roll tin with greaseproof paper .

2   Place the margarine and flours in a saucepan and stir over a moderate heat to make a paste. Gradually stir in the milk until smooth.

3   Remove from the heat and beat in the egg yolks, cheese and spinach. Whisk the egg whites until stiff, then fold into the spinach mixture.

4   Pour into the prepared tin and bake in the oven for 20–25 minutes until a skewer inserted into the centre comes out clean.

5   Remove from the oven and invert on to a clean sheet of greaseproof paper. Cover with a cold, damp tea towel and leave for 1 minute.

6   Peel off the paper and sprinkle with the prawns. Trim the edges and roll up, using the paper to hold the roulade together. Serve at once with wedges of lemon.

Variation

If you want to use fresh spinach, remove the tough stalks from 450 g/1 lb of spinach leaves, wash and drain well, then place in a large saucepan with only the water clinging to the leaves. Place over a moderate heat for a few minutes, shaking occasionally, until the spinach has wilted.

oat pastry

13 g fibre/885 calories

	METRIC	IMPERIAL	AMERICAN
Wholemeal flour	125 g	4½ oz	1 cup
Mornflake oats	50 g	2 oz	½ cup
Soft vegetable margarine or unsalted butter	75 g	3 oz	⅓ cup
Cold water	30 ml	2 tbsp	2 tbsp

1 Put the flour and oats in a bowl, then rub in the margarine or butter until the mixture resembles breadcrumbs. Add just enough cold water to mix to a soft but not sticky dough.

2 To make an Oat Pastry Case, preheat the oven to 200°C/400°F/ gas mark 6 and lightly oil a 20 cm/8 in flan ring.

3 Roll out the pastry on a lightly floured surface, then use to line the flan ring. Cover with greaseproof paper and fill with baking beans.

4 If you are using the flan case for a filling which has to be cooked, bake in the oven for 10 minutes, then remove the paper and beans, fill with the chosen filling and return to the oven for about 20 minutes until both filling and pastry are cooked.

5 To use for an uncooked filling, simply bake for 20 minutes, remove the paper and beans and bake for a further 5 minutes until cooked and golden.

pizza scone

Serves 6   4.5 g fibre/315 calories per portion

	METRIC	IMPERIAL	AMERICAN
Wholemeal flour	225 g	8 oz	2 cups
Oat flour	100 g	4 oz	1 cup
Baking powder	15 ml	1 tbsp	1 tbsp
Soft vegetable margarine	75 g	3 oz	⅓ cup
Mustard powder	5 ml	1 tsp	1 tsp
Gruyère cheese, grated	50 g	2 oz	½ cup
Cayenne	2.5 ml	½ tsp	½ tsp
Lemon juice	10 ml	2 tsp	2 tsp
Skimmed milk	150 ml	¼ pt	⅔ cup
For the topping:			
Corn or soya oil	15 ml	1 tbsp	1 tbsp
Onion, diced	1	1	1
Green pepper, diced	1	1	1
Carrot, grated	1	1	1
Celery stick, sliced	1	1	1
Can of tomatoes	400 g	14 oz	1 large
Freshly ground black pepper			
Dried oregano	5 ml	1 tsp	1 tsp
Dried basil	5 ml	1 tsp	1 tsp
A little potato flour or arrowroot			

1 Preheat the oven to 190°C/375°F/gas mark 5 and lightly oil a baking sheet.

2 Mix the flours and baking powder in a bowl, then rub in the margarine until the mixture resembles fine breadcrumbs. Stir in the mustard, cheese and cayenne. Add the lemon juice to the milk and stir into the flour mixture.

3 Turn on to a lightly floured surface and knead very lightly until the mixture forms a smooth dough. Roll out into a 23cm/7 in circle and place on the baking sheet. Press the centre down lightly so that you have a saucer shape to accommodate the filling more easily.

4 To make the topping, heat the oil in a heavy-based saucepan and fry the onion, pepper, carrot and celery over a low heat for 5 minutes until soft and transparent.

5 Add the tomatoes, black pepper and herbs, and break up the tomatoes with the back of a spoon. Continue to cook for a further 10 minutes, uncovered, until the mixture thickens. If it is still very liquid, thicken with a little potato flour or arrowroot slaked in water.

6 Spoon on to the pizza scone and bake in the oven for 20–25 minutes until cooked through.

swede and carrot gratin

Serves 6   4.5 g fibre/165 calories per serving

	METRIC	IMPERIAL	AMERICAN
Carrots, roughly chopped	450 g	1 lb	1 lb
Swede, roughly chopped	450 g	1 lb	1 lb
Soft vegetable margarine	25 g	1 oz	¼ cup
Free-range eggs	2	2	2
Skimmed milk	60 ml	4 tbsp	4 tbsp
Sea salt and freshly ground black pepper			
Mornflake jumbo oats	75 g	3 oz	¾ cup
Mature Cheddar cheese, grated	50 g	2 oz	½ cup

1 Preheat the oven to 190°C/375°F/gas mark 5 and lightly oil an oven-proof dish.

2 Steam or boil the swede and carrot until just cooked. Drain, if necessary, then mash or liquidise with the margarine, eggs and milk and season to taste with salt and pepper. Place in the dish.

3 Mix the oats and cheese and sprinkle on top.

4 Bake in the oven for 25 minutes, then serve at once.

walnut moussaka

Serves 6   4 g fibre/170 calories per serving

	METRIC	IMPERIAL	AMERICAN
Vegetable oil	15 ml	1 tbsp	1 tbsp
Onions, chopped	2	2	2
Mushrooms, sliced	100 g	4 oz	1 cup
Mornflake oats	50 g	2 oz	½ cup
Walnuts, chopped	100 g	4 oz	1 cup
Wholemeal breadcrumbs	50 g	2 oz	½ cup
Sea salt and freshly ground black pepper			
Can of tomatoes, drained	400 g	14 oz	1 large
Aubergines	2	2	2
For the topping:			
Free-range egg	1	1	1
Oat flour	15 ml	1 tbsp	1 tbsp
Natural yoghurt	150 ml	¼ pt	⅔ cup
Grated cheese	50 g	2 oz	½ cup
Sea salt and freshly ground black pepper			

1 Preheat the oven to 190°C/375°F/gas mark 5 and lightly oil a rectangular ovenproof dish.

2 Heat the oil and gently fry the onions for a few minutes until softened but not browned. Add the mushrooms and cook for 1 minute. Add the oats, walnuts and breadcrumbs, mix well and season with a little sea salt and plenty of black pepper.

3 Slice the aubergines and sprinkle with salt to bring out any bitter juices. Leave for 30 minutes, then rinse thoroughly.

4 Place one-third of the aubergines in a layer in the bottom of the dish. Place half the walnut mixture on top and add the tomatoes. Add another third of the aubergines, the remaining walnut mixture and the last of the aubergines.

5 Mix together the ingredients for the topping and spread over the top. Cook in the oven for 30 minutes until crisp and golden.

parsley scone dumplings

Makes 4   2 g fibre/155 calories per dumpling

	METRIC	IMPERIAL	AMERICAN
Wholemeal flour	50 g	2 oz	½ cup
Oat flour	50 g	2 oz	½ cup
Baking powder	7.5 ml	1½ tsp	1½ tsp
Soft vegetable margarine	40 g	1½ oz	3 tbsp
Chopped fresh parsley	15 ml	1 tbsp	1 tbsp
Freshly ground black pepper			
Cold water	15–30 ml	1–2 tbsp	1–2 tbsp

1 Mix the flours and baking powder in a bowl, then rub in the margarine until the mixture resembles breadcrumbs. Stir in the parsley and pepper and add enough water to mix to a soft dough.

2 Shape into four balls or roll out on a lightly floured surface and cut into four thick scones.

3 Add the dumplings to casseroles or stews and cook for at least 20 minutes.

vegetable burgers

Makes 6   5 g fibre/330 calories per burger

	METRIC	IMPERIAL	AMERICAN
Ground walnuts	100 g	4 oz	1 cup
Ground hazelnuts	100 g	4 oz	1 cup
Wholemeal breadcrumbs	100 g	4 oz	1 cup
Oat flour	50 g	2 oz	½ cup
Dried basil	5 ml	1 tsp	1 tsp
Onion, diced	1 large	1 large	1 large
Free-range egg	1	1	1
Corn, soy or sesame oil	30 ml	2 tbsp	2 tbsp
Mornflake oats	30 ml	2 tbsp	2 tbsp
Sesame seeds	30 ml	2 tbsp	2 tbsp

1   Mix together all the ingredients except for the oats and sesame seeds. Shape into four burgers.

2   Mix together the oats and sesame seeds. Roll the burgers in the mixture until well coated.

3   Cook under a moderate grill for 12 minutes each side until cooked through and browned.

beef burgers

Makes 4   3 g fibre/260 calories per burger

	METRIC	IMPERIAL	AMERICAN
Lean steak, minced	350 g	12 oz	3 cups
Onion, finely chopped	1	1	1
Carrot, grated	1 large	1 large	1 large
Tomato purée	15 ml	1 tbsp	1 tbsp
Thick slice of wholemeal bread, grated to crumbs	1	1	1
Oat flour	30 ml	2 tbsp	2 tbsp
Made mustard	30 ml	2 tbsp	2 tbsp

1   Place all the ingredients in a bowl and combine well. Shape into four burgers.

2   Place under the grill and grill for 10 minutes on each side until cooked through and browned.

traditional moussaka

Serves 6   3 g fibre/360 calories per serving

	METRIC	IMPERIAL	AMERICAN
Vegetable oil	15 ml	1 tbsp	1 tbsp
Onions, finely chopped	2	2	2
Lean minced beef	450 g	1 lb	1 lb
Tomato purée	30 ml	2 tbsp	2 tbsp
Worcestershire sauce	5 ml	1 tsp	1 tsp
Oat flour	75 g	3 oz	¾ cup
Stock	150 ml	¼ pt	⅔ cup
Aubergines	2	2	2
Soft vegetable margarine	50 g	2 oz	¼ cup
Skimmed milk	300 ml	½ pt	1¼ cups
Mature Cheddar, grated	50 g	2 oz	½ cup
Free-range egg, lightly beaten	1	1	1
Can of tomatoes, drained	400 g	14 oz	1 large

1 Preheat the oven to 190°C/375°F/gas mark 5 and lightly oil a large rectangular ovenproof dish.

2 Heat the oil and gently fry the onions for a few minutes until soft. Add the beef and stir until browned. Add the tomato purée and Worcestershire sauce and sprinkle over 30 ml/2 tbsp of the oat flour. Stir well, then add the stock, bring to a simmer and simmer for 15 minutes.

3 Slice the aubergines and blanch in boiling water for 2 minutes, then drain.

4 Place the margarine and remaining oat flour in a saucepan and stir over a moderate heat to make a paste. Gradually stir in the milk to make a smooth sauce, then remove from the heat and stir in the cheese and egg.

5 Place one-third of the aubergines in the bottom of the dish. Place half the meat mixture on top and add the tomatoes. Add another third of the aubergines, the remaining meat mixture and top with the last of the aubergines.

6 Pour over the cheese sauce and bake in the oven for 45 minutes until golden brown.

mushroom and cashew lasagne

Serves 4   5 g fibre/375 calories per serving

	METRIC	IMPERIAL	AMERICAN
Vegetable oil	30 ml	2 tbsp	2 tbsp
Onion, chopped	I	I	I
Leeks, thinly sliced	225 g	8 oz	2 cups
Mushrooms, thinly sliced	225 g	8 oz	2 cups
Cashew nuts, chopped	100 g	4 oz	I cup
Mornflake oats	50 g	2 oz	½ cup
Soy sauce	10 ml	2 tsp	2 tsp
Home-made Oat Pasta (see page 51)	225 g	8 oz	½ lb
Can of chopped tomatoes	400 g	14 oz	I large
White sauce, made with oat flour (see page 42)	300 ml	½ pt	1¼ cups
Low-fat soft cheese	100 g	4 oz	½ cup
Chopped fresh parsley	15 ml	I tbsp	I tbsp

1   Preheat the oven to 190°C/375°F/gas mark 5 and lightly oil a shallow, rectangular ovenproof dish.

2   Heat 15 ml/1 tbsp of the oil and gently fry the onion and leeks for a few minutes until softened but not browned. Stir in the mushrooms, nuts, oats and soy sauce, then remove from the heat.

3   Bring 1.5 litres/2½ pts/6 cups of water and the remaining oil to the boil in a large saucepan. Add a few squares of home-made pasta at a time, and cook for about 6 minutes until just tender. If you use dried pasta, the cooking time will be 10–12 minutes. Drain.

4   Mix together the tomatoes, white sauce and cheese.

5   Place half the cashew sauce in the dish and cover with a layer of pasta, then a layer of tomato and cheese sauce. Repeat, ending with a layer of sauce. Bake in the oven for 30 minutes. Serve sprinkled with a little chopped parsley.

home-made oat pasta

Serves 4   26 g fibre/160 calories per serving

	METRIC	IMPERIAL	AMERICAN
Wholemeal flour	225 g	8 oz	2 cups
Oat flour	100 g	4 oz	1 cup
Free-range eggs	3	3	3
Oil	15 ml	1 tbsp	1 tbsp
Water	30 ml	2 tbsp	2 tbsp
Fine sea salt	5 ml	1 tsp	1 tsp

1 Place the flours in a bowl and make a well in the centre. Stir in the remaining ingredients and knead together to form a dough. Knead thoroughly, adding a little more flour if necessary. Cover and leave to rest for 1 hour.

2 Quarter the dough and pass it at least twice through a pasta machine or roll it out thinly by hand and cut into appropriate shapes, such as 7 cm/ 3 in squares for lasagne, or long strips for tagliatelle.

leek pie

Serves 4   5.5 g fibre/280 calories per serving

	METRIC	IMPERIAL	AMERICAN
For the filling:			
Leeks	450 g	1 lb	4 cups
Free-range eggs	2	2	2
Mature Cheddar cheese, grated	50 g	2 oz	½ cup
Natural yoghurt	150 ml	¼ pt	⅔ cup
Sea salt and freshly ground black pepper			
For the pastry:			
Wholemeal flour	75 g	3 oz	¾ cup
Mornflake oats	25 g	1 oz	¼ cup
A pinch of salt			
Soft vegetable margarine	50 g	2 oz	¼ cup
Cold water	15–30 ml	1–2 tbsp	1–2 tbsp
A little milk or beaten egg, to glaze			

1   Preheat the oven to 200°C/400°F/gas mark 6 and lightly oil a deep pie dish.

2   Trim the leeks, leaving 2.5 cm/1 in of green at the top. Cut into 2.5 cm/1 in slices and wash thoroughly. Plunge into boiling water or steam for 5 minutes. Drain and place in the base of the pie dish.

3   Beat the eggs with the cheese and yoghurt and season with salt and pepper. Pour over the leeks.

4   To make the pastry, mix the flour, oats and salt in a bowl, then rub in the margarine until the mixture resembles breadcrumbs. Add enough cold water to mix to a soft dough. Turn on to a lightly floured surface and roll out to 2.5 cm/1 in larger than the dish.

5   Cut off a narrow strip of pastry. Moisten the rim of the pie dish and gently press the strip round the rim. Brush with water, then carefully lift the pastry over the pie dish and place on top. Trim and flute the edges of the pastry with the back of a knife. Roll out the pastry trimmings and use to decorate the top of the pie. Brush with milk or beaten egg to glaze.

6   Bake in the oven for 30 minutes until golden brown.

oat vegetable pie

Serves 4   9 g fibre/280 calories per portion

	METRIC	IMPERIAL	AMERICAN
Swede, diced	225 g	8 oz	2 cups
Carrots, diced	225 g	8 oz	2 cups
Shelled or frozen peas	225 g	8 oz	2 cups
Chopped fresh parsley	30 ml	2 tbsp	2 tbsp
Vegetable stock	300 ml	½ pt	1¼ cups
For the topping: Unsalted butter or soft vegetable margarine	25 g	1 oz	2 tbsp
Potato, boiled	1 large	1 large	1 large
Mature English cheddar, grated	50 g	2 oz	½ cup
Mornflake oats	50 g	2 oz	½ cup
Wholemeal flour	100 g	4 oz	1 cup
Sea salt and freshly ground black pepper			
Water	30–45 ml	2–3 tbsp	2–3 tbsp
Skimmed milk	5 ml	1 tsp	1 tsp

1 Preheat the oven to 200°C/400°F/gas mark 5 and lightly oil an oven-proof dish.

2 Steam or boil the swede and carrots for 5 minutes. Blanch the peas, if fresh, for 1 minute. Mix the vegetables with the parsley and stock and place in dish.

3 To make the topping, mash together the butter or margarine and potato. Mix together the cheese, oats and flour and season with salt and pepper and add to the potato. Add enough water to form a soft dough.

4 Roll out the dough and place over the vegetables to form a crust. Glaze with the milk.

5 Bake in the oven for 30 minutes until golden.

mushroom fish pie

Serves 4   1.5 g fibre/370 calories per serving

	METRIC	IMPERIAL	AMERICAN
1 quantity of Oat Pastry (see page 43)			
For the filling:			
Oil	15 ml	1 tbsp	1 tbsp
Onion, diced	1 large	1 large	1 large
Mushrooms, sliced	175 g	6 oz	1½ cups
Oat flour	15 ml	1 tbsp	1 tbsp
Skimmed milk	150 ml	¼ pt	⅔ cup
Cod fillet, or other white fish, skinned and cut into strips	450 g	1 lb	4 cups
Freshly ground black pepper			
A little milk or beaten egg, to glaze			

1 Make the pastry and preheat the oven to 200°C/400°F/gas mark 6.

2 Heat the oil and gently fry the onion until transparent. Stir in the mushrooms, cover and cook for 5 minutes. Stir in the flour, then gradually stir in the milk to form a thick sauce.

3 Add the fish, season with pepper and cook for 2 minutes, then turn into an ovenproof dish.

4 Roll the pastry into a circle large enough to cover the dish. Cut strips from the excess and place around the rim. Brush with water and place the pastry lid on top. Flute the edges of the pastry to seal with the strips and decorate the top with shapes cut from the trimmings. Glaze with milk or beaten egg.

5 Bake in the oven for 30 minutes until golden.

parsnip croquettes

Makes 8   3.5 g fibre/120 calories per croquette

	METRIC	IMPERIAL	AMERICAN
Parsnips, roughly chopped	900 g	2 lb	8 cups
Unsalted butter or soft vegetable margarine	50 g	2 oz	¼ cup
Mature cheese, grated	100 g	4 oz	1 cup
Wholemeal breadcrumbs	100 g	4 oz	1 cup
Mornflake oats	50 g	2 oz	½ cup
Mustard powder	5 ml	1 tsp	1 tsp

1 Preheat the oven to 190°C/375°F/gas mark 5 and lightly oil a baking sheet.

2 Steam or boil the parsnips until soft, then drain well.

3 Mash or liquidise the parsnips with the butter or margarine and most of the cheese. Stir in the breadcrumbs and leave until cool enough to handle. Shape into croquettes.

4 Mix together the oats, the remainder of the cheese and the mustard and roll the croquettes in the mixture.

5 Place on the baking sheet and cook in the oven for 20 minutes, turning once, until golden.

braised meatballs and vegetables

Serves 6   1.5 g fibre/95 calories per portion

	METRIC	IMPERIAL	AMERICAN
For the meatballs:			
Minced steak	450 g	1 lb	4 cups
Wholemeal breadcrumbs	25 g	1 oz	¼ cup
Oat flour	25 g	1 oz	2 tbsp
Onion, minced or grated	1	1	1
Free-range egg	1	1	1
Ground allspice	5 ml	1 tsp	1 tsp
Salt and freshly ground black pepper			
For the vegetable base:			
Vegetable oil	10 ml	2 tsp	2 tsp
Celery sticks, cut into 2.5 cm/1 in pieces	6	6	6
Carrots, thinly sliced	2	2	2
Onion, finely chopped	1 large	1 large	1 large
Vegetable stock	450 ml	¾ pt	2 cups
Lemon juice	5 ml	1 tsp	1 tsp

1 Preheat the oven to 200°C/400°F/gas mark 6.

2 Stir together all the meatball ingredients and form into balls.

3 Lightly fry the meatballs in a smear of oil to seal the outsides.

4 Heat the oil and gently fry the vegetables for 3 minutes, then transfer to an ovenproof dish. Pour over the stock and lemon juice and season with salt and pepper.

5 Place the meatballs on top of the vegetables and stock and bake in the oven for 40 minutes until tender.

eastern fishcakes

Serves 4   0.5 g fibre/195 calories per portion

	METRIC	IMPERIAL	AMERICAN
Mackerel, filleted, skinned and flaked	1	1	1
Coley or cod fillet, skinned and flaked	175 g	6 oz	1½ cups
Cooked, mashed potato	100 g	4 oz	1 cup
Garlic clove, crushed	1	1	1
Onion, grated	1	1	1
Free-range egg, lightly beaten	1	1	1
Freshly ground black pepper	5 ml	1 tsp	1 tsp
Vegetable oil	10 ml	2 tsp	2 tsp
For the sauce: Tomato purée	30 ml	2 tbsp	2 tbsp
Onion, grated	1	1	1
Red pepper, finely diced	1	1	1
Juice of 1 lemon			
Ground cumin	10 ml	2 tsp	2 tsp
Red wine vinegar	10 ml	2 tsp	2 tsp
Demerara sugar	5 ml	1 tsp	1 tsp
Water	600 ml	1 pt	2½ cups
Oat flour	5 ml	1 tsp	1 tsp
Vegetable oil	10 ml	2 tsp	2 tsp
Crisp green salad, to serve			

1   Mix together all the fishcake ingredients except the oil and form into eight balls.

2   Heat the oil and lightly fry the fishcakes until browned on all sides.

3   Mix together all the ingredients for the sauce except the flour and oil.

4   Place the oat flour and oil in a saucepan and stir over a moderate heat to make a roux. Gradually stir in the sauce ingredients and cook for 2 minutes, then carefully drop in the fishcakes. Cover the pan and cook over a low heat for 30 minutes, stirring occasionally to keep the sauce smooth and prevent it sticking to the bottom of the pan.

5   Serve with a crisp green salad.

chicken chervil croquettes

Makes 16   0.5 g fibre/60 calories per croquette

	METRIC	IMPERIAL	AMERICAN
For the oatcrunch coating:			
Wholemeal breadcrumbs	50 g	2 oz	½ cup
Mornflake oats	25 g	1 oz	¼ cup
Sesame seeds	25 g	1 oz	¼ cup
For the croquettes:			
4 boneless chicken breasts	450 g	1 lb	1 lb
Low-fat curd cheese	225 g	8 oz	2 cups
Grated rind and juice of lemon	½	½	½
Chopped fresh chervil	15 ml	1 tbsp	1 tbsp
Coarse-grain made mustard	5 ml	1 tsp	1 tsp
Free-range egg whites	2	2	2

1   Mix together all the coating ingredients and place in a heavy-based frying pan. Toss over a low heat until evenly browned.

2   Preheat the oven to 200°C/400°F/gas mark 6 and oil a baking sheet.

3   Mince the chicken and mix with the cheese, lemon rind and juice, chervil and mustard and beat to a purée. This can be done in a food processor.

4   Whisk the egg whites until stiff, then gradually fold them in.

5 Mould into croquettes and roll in the oatcrunch coating. Place on the prepared tray and cook in the oven for 20 minutes, turning once.

spiced crispy chicken

Serves 4   1.5 g fibre/525 calories per serving

	METRIC	IMPERIAL	AMERICAN
Chicken legs	4	4	4
Free-range egg, beaten	1	1	1
Mornflake oats	100 g	4 oz	1 cup
Celery salt	5 ml	1 tsp	1 tsp
Garlic powder (to taste)			
Paprika	2.5 ml	½ tsp	½ tsp

1 Preheat the oven to 190°C/375°F/gas mark 5 and oil an ovenproof dish.

2 Remove the skin from the chicken and coat in the beaten egg. Season the oats with celery salt, garlic powder and paprika, then roll the chicken in the mixture. Place in the dish and sprinkle any extra oats over the top.

3 Bake in the oven for 1 hour until tender and crisp.

sweet and sour sauce

Serves 4   0 g fibre/20 calories per serving

	METRIC	IMPERIAL	AMERICAN
Tomato purée	15 ml	1 tbsp	1 tbsp
Soy sauce	30 ml	2 tbsp	2 tbsp
Wine, cider or sherry vinegar	15 ml	1 tbsp	1 tbsp
Water	30 ml	2 tbsp	2 tbsp
Demerara sugar	10 ml	2 tsp	2 tsp
Arrowroot or potato flour (optional)	10 ml	2 tsp	2 tsp

1 Place the ingredients in a saucepan and dissolve over a low heat, stirring.

2 If you prefer a thicker sauce, blend the arrowroot or potato flour to a paste with a little water, stir into the sauce and simmer until thickened.

SNACKS

spinach and yoghurt soup

Serves 6   3 g fibre/80 calories per serving

	METRIC	IMPERIAL	AMERICAN
Vegetable oil	10 ml	2 tsp	2 tsp
Onion, chopped	1 large	1 large	1 large
Garlic clove, crushed	1	1	1
Spinach, cooked and chopped, or frozen	300 g	10 oz	2½ cups
Chicken or vegetable stock	900 ml	1½ pts	3¾ cups
Oat flour	50 g	2 oz	½ cup
Skimmed milk	30 ml	2 tbsp	2 tbsp
Freshly grated nutmeg			
Sea salt and freshly ground black pepper			
Free-range egg yolk	1	1	1
Natural yoghurt	150 ml	¼ pt	⅔ cup
Extra yoghurt or croûtons, to serve (optional)			

1 Heat the oil and gently fry the onion and garlic for a few minutes until softened but not browned. Add the spinach and stock, bring to the boil, cover and cook for 10 minutes.

2 Purée the soup in a liquidiser, then return it to the pan.

3 Mix the oat flour with the milk and add to the pan with nutmeg, salt and pepper to taste. Bring to the boil, stirring continuously, and simmer for 5 minutes. Remove from the heat and leave to cool slightly.

4 Blend the egg yolk with the yoghurt and stir into the soup.

5 Serve the soup with an extra swirl of yoghurt and toasted croûtons for special occasions.

savoury snaps

Makes 24 biscuits 1 g fibre/65 calories per biscuit

	METRIC	IMPERIAL	AMERICAN
Wholemeal flour	175 g	6 oz	1½ cups
Oat flour	50 g	2 oz	½ cup
Soft vegetable margarine	50 g	2 oz	¼ cup
Sesame seeds	30 ml	2 tbsp	2 tbsp
Caraway seeds	5 ml	1 tsp	1 tsp
Cayenne	2.5 ml	½ tsp	½ tsp
A pinch of sea salt			
Free-range egg	1	1	1
Skimmed milk	45–60 ml	3–4 tbsp	3–4 tbsp

1 Preheat the oven to 190°C/375°F/gas mark 5 and lightly oil two baking sheets.

2 Mix together the flours, then rub in the margarine until the mixture resembles breadcrumbs. Stir in the remaining ingredients with enough milk to form a soft dough.

3 Roll out the dough to 5 mm/¼ in thick and cut into rectangular biscuits. Arrange on the baking sheets.

4 Bake in the oven for 15–20 minutes until golden.

oatcake fingers

Makes 24   0.5 g fibre/55 calories per finger

	METRIC	IMPERIAL	AMERICAN
Mornflake oatmeal	200 g	7 oz	1¾ cups
Oat flour	75 g	3 oz	¾ cup
Baking powder	5 ml	I tsp	I tsp
Soft vegetable margarine	50 g	2 oz	¼ cup
Boiling water	30–45 ml	2–3 tbsp	2–3 tbsp

I Preheat the oven to 190°C/375°F/gas mark 5 and lightly oil two baking sheets.

2 Mix the oatmeal, oat flour and baking powder in a bowl.

3 Melt the margarine in a saucepan, then stir into the dry ingredients. Gradually add enough boiling water to make a soft but not sticky dough, being careful not to add too much. Turn on to a lightly floured surface and knead until the dough is firm enough to roll out.

4 Roll the dough into a rectangle. Trim the edges and cut into fingers. Slip a palette knife under the fingers and carefully lift them on to the baking sheets.

5 Bake in the oven for 10–15 minutes until golden brown.

yoghurt treat

Serves 1 3.5 g fibre/210 calories per portion

	METRIC	IMPERIAL	AMERICAN
Fresh dates, stoned and quartered	4	4	4
Natural yoghurt	150 ml	¼ pt	⅔ cup
Clear honey	5 ml	1 tsp	1 tsp
Family Favourite Granola (see page 26)	15 ml	1 tbsp	1 tbsp

1 Mix the dates and yoghurt and place in a serving glass. Drizzle over the honey.

2 Top with granola and serve at once.

oat drop scones

Makes 12 0.5g/60 calories per scone

	METRIC	IMPERIAL	AMERICAN
Mornflake oats	100 g	4 oz	1 cup
A pinch of salt			
Free-range egg	1	1	1
Skimmed milk	300 ml	½ pt	1¼ cups
Butter or soft vegetable margarine, melted	25 g	1 oz	2 tbsp

1 Mix together the oats and salt in a bowl and make a well in the centre.

2 Break in the egg, then gradually add the milk, stirring to make a thick batter. Stir in the melted butter and leave to stand for 1 hour.

3 Heat a lightly oiled non-stick pan and cook spoonfuls of the batter for 3 minutes on each side until golden.

4 Serve hot with a cooked breakfast.

cheese and onion pancakes

Makes 12   1 g fibre/65 calories per pancake

	METRIC	IMPERIAL	AMERICAN
1 quantity of Oat Pancake Batter (see page 38)			
Potato, grated	1	1	1
Onion, grated	1	1	1
Red Leicester cheese, grated	50 g	2 oz	½ cup
Vegetable oil	30 ml	2 tbsp	2 tbsp

1 Make the batter in the usual way, then stir in the potato, onion and cheese.

2 Heat a little of the oil in a frying pan, then add tablespoonfuls of the batter mixture and cook for 1–2 minutes on each side until golden. Remove from the pan and keep hot while you cook the remaining batter. Serve hot.

blinis

Makes 24   1 g fibre/55 calories per blini

	METRIC	IMPERIAL	AMERICAN
Wholemeal flour	350 g	10 oz	2½ cups
Oat flour	50 g	2 oz	½ cup
Fresh yeast	15 g	½ oz	1 tbsp
Lukewarm water	300 ml	½ pt	1¼ cups
Unsalted butter, melted	25 g	1 oz	2 tbsp
Free-range eggs, separated	2	2	2
Lukewarm skimmed milk	300 ml	½ pt	1¼ cups
Vegetable oil	30 ml	2 tbsp	2 tbsp

1   Mix the flours and place half in a bowl.

2   Crumble the yeast into the water and stir into the flour. Mix well, cover and leave in a warm place for 30 minutes until doubled in volume.

3   Blend in the remaining flour, the butter and beaten egg yolks. Beat the mixture until smooth. Stir in the warmed milk and beat well. Cover and leave to rise as before.

4   Whisk the egg whites until stiff and fold into the batter.

5   Heat a little of the oil in a frying pan and put tablespoonfuls of the batter into the pan to make 10 cm/4 in blinis. Cook for 1 minute on each side.

6   Serve with savoury sauces, grated vegetables or sprinkled with a little cheese, or topped with soured cream and caviar.

Cook's note
Remember you can make your own oat flour by grinding some Mornflake oats or oatmeal in a food processor (see page 16).

crunchy bars

Makes 12   2 g fibre/220 calories per bar

	METRIC	IMPERIAL	AMERICAN
Soft vegetable margarine	150 g	5 oz	⅔ cup
Clear honey	45 ml	3 tbsp	3 tbsp
Almond essence	2 drops	2 drops	2 drops
Mornflake oats	225 g	8 oz	2 cups
Flaked almonds	25 g	1 oz	2 tbsp
Mornflake Farmhouse Wheatbran	50 g	2 oz	1 cup
Sunflower seeds	25 g	1 oz	¼ cup
Sesame seeds	25 g	1 oz	¼ cup
Sultanas or raisins	50 g	2 oz	⅓ cup

1 Preheat the oven to 190°C/375°F/gas mark 5 and lightly oil a 20 cm/ 8 in square baking tin.

2 Melt the margarine and honey in a saucepan. Remove from the heat and add the almond essence.

3 Place the remaining ingredients in a bowl, pour on the margarine and stir thoroughly to mix. Press the mixture firmly into the prepared tin.

4 Bake in the oven for 20 minutes. Remove from oven and leave to cool slightly, then cut into fingers and leave in the tin until completely cold.

cheese crackers

Makes 50   0.5 g fibre/40 calories per cracker

	METRIC	IMPERIAL	AMERICAN
Mature Cheddar cheese, grated	100 g	4 oz	I cup
Grated Parmesan cheese	30 ml	2 tbsp	2 tbsp
Wholemeal flour	175 g	6 oz	I½ cups
Oat flour	75 g	3 oz	¾ cup
Mustard powder	2.5 ml	½ tsp	½ tsp
Soft vegetable margarine	75 g	3 oz	⅓ cup
Cold water	30–45 ml	2–3 tbsp	2–3 tbsp

I Preheat the oven to 200°C/400°F/gas mark 6 and lightly oil several baking sheets.

2 Mix together the cheeses, flour and mustard. Rub in the margarine until the mixture resembles breadcrumbs. Add just enough cold water to mix to a soft but not sticky dough.

3 Halve the dough, then roll each piece out thinly on a lightly floured work surface. Cut into biscuits with a knife or pastry cutter and place them on the trays.

4 Bake in the oven for 10 minutes until golden, then transfer to wire cooling trays to cool and harden.

scotch eggs

Makes 4   4 g fibre/250 calories each

	METRIC	IMPERIAL	AMERICAN
Vegetable oil	10 ml	2 tsp	2 tsp
Onions, chopped	2	2	2
Ground hazelnuts	50 g	2 oz	½ cup
Wholemeal breadcrumbs	50 g	2 oz	½ cup
Mornflake oats	50 g	2 oz	½ cup
Carrots, grated	2	2	2
Sesame seeds	15 ml	1 tbsp	1 tbsp
A pinch of dried marjoram			
A pinch of mustard powder			
Tomato ketchup	15 ml	1 tbsp	1 tbsp
Free-range egg, lightly beaten	1	1	1
Free-range eggs, hard-boiled and shelled	4	4	4

1 Preheat the oven to 190°C/375°F/gas mark 5 and lightly oil a baking sheet.

2 Heat the oil and gently fry the onions for a few minutes until transparent.

3 Mix together the hazelnuts, breadcrumbs, oats, carrots, sesame seeds and flavourings. Stir in the onion, ketchup and lightly beaten egg to make a soft mixture.

4 Gently mould a quarter of the mixture around each of the hard-boiled eggs and place on the baking sheet.

5 Bake in the oven for 20–25 minutes until golden.

cheese flapjacks

Makes 14   1 g fibre/125 calories

	METRIC	IMPERIAL	AMERICAN
Mornflake jumbo oats	225 g	8 oz	2 cups
Mature Cheddar cheese, grated	100 g	4 oz	1 cup
Soft vegetable margarine	75 g	3 oz	⅓ cup
Made mustard	5 ml	1 tsp	1 tsp
Natural yoghurt	150 ml	¼ pt	⅔ cup
Free-range egg, beaten	1	1	1
Freshly ground black pepper			

1 Preheat the oven to 180°C/350°F/gas mark 4 and lightly oil a 23 cm/
   9 in square cake tin.

2 Mix the oats and cheese in a large bowl. Melt the margarine in a
   saucepan, then stir it into the oats with the mustard, yoghurt and egg and
   season with pepper. Press gently into the prepared tin.

3 Bake in the oven for 25–30 minutes until golden brown. Remove from
   the oven and cut into slices, then leave to cool in the tin.

cheese scones

Makes 6   2 g fibre/115 calories per scone

	METRIC	IMPERIAL	AMERICAN
Oat flour	25 g	1 oz	¼ cup
Wholemeal flour	75 g	3 oz	¾ cup
Baking powder	5 ml	1 tsp	1 tsp
Mustard powder	2.5 ml	½ tsp	½ tsp
Paprika	1.25 ml	¼ tsp	¼ tsp
Soft vegetable margarine or unsalted butter	25 g	1 oz	2 tbsp
Cheddar cheese, grated	50 g	2 oz	½ cup
Skimmed milk	15–30 ml	1–2 tbsp	1–2 tbsp
Skimmed milk or beaten egg, to glaze			
Mornflake oats	30 ml	2 tbsp	2 tbsp
Paprika	2.5 ml	½ tsp	½ tsp

1 Preheat the oven to 220°C/425°F/gas mark 7 and lightly oil a baking sheet.

2 Mix the flours, baking powder, mustard powder and paprika in a bowl, then rub in the margarine or butter until the mixture resembles breadcrumbs. Stir in the grated cheese. Gradually blend in enough milk to make a soft and pliable dough.

3 Roll out the dough on a lightly floured surface to about 2 cm/¾ in thick and cut into 5 cm/2 in rounds with a pastry cutter. Place on the baking sheet and brush the tops with milk or beaten egg. Sprinkle with the oats and paprika.

4 Bake in the oven for 10–12 minutes until risen and golden on top.

herb scones

Makes 6   1.5 g fibre/100 calories per scone.

	METRIC	IMPERIAL	AMERICAN
Wholemeal flour	75 g	3 oz	¾ cup
Oat flour	25 g	1 oz	2 tbsp
Baking powder	5 ml	1 tsp	1 tsp
Soft vegetable margarine	40 g	1½ oz	⅓ cup
Chopped fresh sage, thyme, parsley or other herb	10 ml	2 tsp	2 tsp
Skimmed milk	75 ml	5 tbsp	5 tbsp

1 Preheat the oven to 220°C/425°F/gas mark 7 and lightly oil a baking sheet.

2 Mix the flours and baking powder in a bowl, then rub in the margarine until the mixture resembles breadcrumbs. Stir in the herbs and just enough of the milk to make a soft dough. Knead lightly until firm enough to roll out.

3 Roll out the dough on a lightly floured surface to about 1 cm/½ in thick and cut into 5 cm/2 in rounds with a pastry cutter. Place on the baking sheet and brush the top of the scones with the remaining milk.

4 Bake in the oven for 10 minutes until risen and firm. Serve hot or cold.

71

DESSERTS

blackberry and apple crumble

Serves 4   8.5 g fibre/340 calories per portion

	METRIC	IMPERIAL	AMERICAN
Cooking apples	450 g	1 lb	1 lb
Lemon	1	1	1
Blackberries	225 g	8 oz	2 cups
Wholemeal flour	50 g	2 oz	½ cup
Mornflake oats	50 g	2 oz	½ cup
Unsalted butter or soft vegetable margarine	75 g	3 oz	⅓ cup
Stoned dates, finely chopped	50 g	2 oz	⅓ cup
Sunflower seeds	25 g	1 oz	¼ cup

1 Preheat the oven to 200°C/400°F/gas mark 6 and lightly oil an ovenproof dish.

2 Core and slice the unpeeled apples and dress with lemon juice to prevent browning. Place in a saucepan with the blackberries over a low heat and bring to a simmer, cover and simmer for 5 minutes. Turn the fruit into the dish.

3 Mix together the flour and oats, then rub in the fat until the mixture resembles breadcrumbs. Stir in the dates and sunflower seeds, then sprinkle the mixture over the fruit.

4 Bake in the oven for 25 minutes.

lemon curd tart

Serves 6   3 g/440 calories per portion

	METRIC	IMPERIAL	AMERICAN
For the lemon curd:			
Grated rind and juice of lemons	2 large	2 large	2 large
Muscovado sugar	100 g	4 oz	½ cup
Unsalted butter	75 g	3 oz	⅓ cup
Free-range eggs, lightly beaten	2	2	2
For the pastry:			
Wholemeal flour	100 g	4 oz	I cup
Oat flour	50 g	2 oz	½ cup
Ground almonds	50 g	2 oz	½ cup
Soft vegetable margarine	75 g	3 oz	⅓ cup
Grated rind of lemon	I	I	I
Water	45–60 ml	3–4 tbsp	3–4 tbsp

Lemon, sliced, to garnish (optional)

I   To make the lemon curd, place all the ingredients in the top of a double boiler or in a basin in a saucepan of hot water. Stir over a medium heat for about 10–15 minutes until the mixture melts and thickens. Do not allow the mixtxure to boil otherwise it will curdle.

2   Cover with a sheet of greaseproof paper and leave to cool.

3   Preheat the oven to 200°C/400°F/gas mark 6 and lightly oil a 20 cm/ 8 in flan ring.

4   Mix the flours and ground almonds in a bowl, then rub in the margarine until the mixture resembles breadcrumbs. Stir in the lemon rind and enough of the water to make a soft dough.

5   Roll out the dough on a floured surface and use to line the flan ring. Cover with greaseproof paper and fill with baking beans and bake blind for 25 minutes. Remove from the oven and leave to cool.

6   Fill with lemon curd and garnish with lemon slices, if liked.

fruit tart
Serve 4   4 g fibre/255 calories per serving

	METRIC	IMPERIAL	AMERICAN
Wholemeal flour	100 g	4 oz	1 cup
Oat flour	50 g	2 oz	½ cup
Soft vegetable margarine	50 g	2 oz	¼ cup
Water	15–30 ml	2–3 tbsp	2–3 tbsp
Cox's or other eating apples, cored and sliced	450 g	1 lb	4 cups
Clear honey or no-added-sugar jam	30 ml	2 tbsp	2 tbsp
For the topping: Soft vegetable margarine	25 g	1 oz	2 tbsp
Clear honey	15 ml	1 tbsp	1 tbsp
Mornflake oats	50 g	2 oz	½ cup

1 Preheat the oven to 190°C/375°F/gas mark 5 and lightly oil a 20 cm/ 8 in flan ring.

2 Mix the flours in a bowl, then rub in the fat until the mixture resembles breadcrumbs. Add enough water to bind to a soft dough.

3 Roll out the pastry on a lightly floured surface and use to line the prepared flan ring. Cover with greaseproof paper and fill with baking beans and bake blind for 10 minutes. Remove from the oven and remove the paper and beans.

4 Bring a large pan of water to the boil, add the apple slices and blanch for 2 minutes, then drain. Arrange the slices in the prepared pastry case and brush with the honey and jam.

5 To prepare the topping, melt the margarine and honey, then remove from the heat and stir in the oats. Sprinkle the mixture around the edges of the prepared flan.

6 Bake in the oven for 20 minutes.

fruit salad

Serves 4   2.5 g fibre/200 calories per portion

	METRIC	IMPERIAL	AMERICAN
Apple	1	1	1
Pear	1	1	1
Juice of lemon	½	½	½
Banana, sliced	1	1	1
Orange juice	150 ml	¼ pt	⅔ cup
Green grapes, halved and seeded	175 g	6 oz	1½ cups
Dried figs, thinly sliced	4	4	4
Family Favourite Granola (see page 26)			

1 Quarter, core and dice the apple and pear without peeling them. Toss in the lemon juice.

2 Add the banana, orange juice, grapes and figs.

3 Just before serving, scatter a little granola on top of the fruit salad.

75

dutch apple cake

Serves 6   10 g fibre/450 calories per portion

	METRIC	IMPERIAL	AMERICAN
Wholemeal flour	175 g	6 oz	1½ cups
Oat flour	50 g	2 oz	½ cup
Baking powder	5 ml	1 tsp	1 tsp
Unsalted butter or soft vegetable margarine	150 g	5 oz	⅔ cup
Free-range eggs, separated	2	2	2
Juice of lemon	1	1	1
Cooking apples, quartered, cored and sliced	900 g	2 lb	8 cups
Water	45 ml	3 tbsp	3 tbsp
No-need-to-soak dried apricots	175 g	6 oz	1 cup
Raisins	100 g	4 oz	⅔ cup
Ground cinnamon	5 ml	1 tsp	1 tsp
Ground almonds	50 g	2 oz	½ cup

1 Preheat the oven to 180°C/350°F/gas mark 4 and lightly oil a 23 cm/ 9 in cake tin.

2 Mix the flours and baking powder in a bowl, then rub in the butter or margarine until the mixture resembles breadcrumbs. Lightly beat the egg yolks, add to the pastry with a tablespoonful of lemon juice and bind to a soft pastry.

3 Roll out three-quarters of the pastry on a lightly floured surface and use to line the tin. Roll the remainder ready for use as a lid.

4 Cook the apples and water over a low heat for 5 minutes, stirring occasionally, then drain.

5 Put the apricots in another pan, almost cover with water, boil for about 5 minutes, then drain.

6 Fill the prepared pastry case with layers of apple, apricots and raisins. Mix together the cinnamon and ground almonds and sprinkle on top. Brush the edges of the pie with egg white and place the pastry lid in position. Brush with the remaining egg white.

7 Bake in the oven for 45–50 minutes until golden.

hot fruit compôte

Serves 4   5 g fibre/325 calories per portion

	METRIC	IMPERIAL	AMERICAN
Water	600 ml	1 pt	2½ cups
Clear honey	15 ml	1 tbsp	1 tbsp
Cinnamon stick	1	1	1
Freshly grated nutmeg	2.5 ml	½ tsp	½ tsp
Cloves	2	2	2
Grated rind and juice of lemon	1	1	1
No-need-to-soak dried apricots	100 g	4 oz	⅔ cup
Dried apple rings	100 g	4 oz	⅔ cup
Can of peaches in fruit juice	400 g	14 oz	1 large
Sultanas	50 g	2 oz	⅓ cup

Family Favourite Granola (see page 26) or natural yoghurt, to serve

1 Place the water, honey, spices and lemon rind and juice in saucepan and bring to the boil. Add the apricots and apples, cover and simmer for 20 minutes.

2 Add the peaches and sultanas and continue to cook for a further 10 minutes.

3 Serve hot, offering the granola or yoghurt in a separate dish.

apple strudel ice-cream

Makes 8 scoops   1.5 g fibre/85 calories per scoop

	METRIC	IMPERIAL	AMERICAN
Walnuts, chopped	50 g	2 oz	½ cup
Cooking apples, peeled, cored and sliced	350 g	12 oz	3 cups
Juice of lemon	½	½	½
Concentrated apple juice	30 ml	2 tbsp	2 tbsp
Oat flour	50 g	2 oz	½ cup
Ground cinnamon	5 ml	1 tsp	1 tsp
Natural yoghurt	150 ml	¼ pt	⅔ cup
Free-range egg whites	2	2	2

1 Place the walnuts, apple, lemon juice and apple juice in a saucepan, cover and cook over a low heat for about 10 minutes to make a purée. Remove from the heat.

2 Beat in the oat flour and cinnamon, then leave to cool.

3 Fold in the yoghurt. Whisk the egg whites until stiff and fold them into the mixture.

4 Place in a shallow container and freeze for about 2 hours. When nearly frozen, break up with a fork and mash. Return to the freezer in a container that is deep enough to allow scoops to be taken.

5 Remove the ice-cream from the freezer 20–30 minutes before serving to allow it to soften.

apple strudel crêpes

Makes 8   3 g fibre/120 calories per crêpe

	METRIC	IMPERIAL	AMERICAN
1 quantity of Oat Pancakes (see page 38)			
Cooking apples, peeled, cored and sliced	350 g	12 oz	3 cups
Juice of lemon	½	½	½
Sultanas	50g	2 oz	⅓ cup
Walnuts, chopped	25 g	1 oz	¼ cup
Ground cinnamon	2.5 ml	½ tsp	½ tsp
Water	60 ml	4 tbsp	4 tbsp
Wholemeal breadcrumbs	50 g	2 oz	½ cup

1 Prepare and cook the pancakes and keep them warm.

2 Toss the apple slices in the lemon juice and place in a stainless steel saucepan with the sultanas, walnuts, cinnamon and water. Bring to the boil, cover and simmer for 15 minutes, stirring from time to time and adding a little more water if necessary.

3 Remove from the heat and stir in the breadcrumbs. Spread on to the crêpes, roll up and serve.

crêpes suzette

Makes 8   2 g fibre/190 calories per portion

	METRIC	IMPERIAL	AMERICAN
I quantity of Oat Pancakes (see page 38)			
Juicy oranges	2 large	2 large	2 large
Juicy lemons	2 large	2 large	2 large
Cointreau or Grand Marnier	30 ml	2 tbsp	2 tbsp
Demerara sugar	30 ml	2 tbsp	2 tbsp

1   Prepare and cook the pancakes and keep them warm.

2   Squeeze the juice from the fruit and mix with the liqueur and sugar.

3   Fold the crêpes into quarters and place in a large frying pan. Pour over the juice and heat through, shaking the pan gently.

4   Flambé, if liked, by adding a little extra liqueur and setting light to the mixture.

banana crêpes

Makes 8   2 g fibre/80 calories per pancake

	METRIC	IMPERIAL	AMERICAN
Grated rind of lemon	I	I	I
I quantity of Oat Pancake batter (see page 38)			
A pinch of ground cinnamon			
A little vegetable oil			
Bananas, thinly sliced	2	2	2

1   Stir the lemon rind into the basic batter and add a pinch of cinnamon.

2   Heat a large pancake pan and lightly smear with oil. Spread about 45 ml/3 tbsp of the batter evenly over the base of the pan, add a few banana slices. Cook on one side for 1–1½ minutes, then slip a fish slice under the pancake and turn to cook briefly on the banana side.

3   Cook the remaining pancakes in the same way.

marzipan franzipan

Serves 8   3 g fibre/200 calories per portion

	METRIC	IMPERIAL	AMERICAN
For the pastry:			
Wholemeal flour	50 g	2 oz	½ cup
Oat flour	50 g	2 oz	½ cup
Soft vegetable margarine	50 g	2 oz	½ cup
Water	15–30 ml	1–2 tbsp	1–2 tbsp
For the filling:			
Pears, peeled, cored and halved	3 small	3 small	3 small
Raw sugar marzipan	50 g	2 oz	¼ cup
Soft vegetable margarine	50 g	2 oz	¼ cup
Free-range egg, lightly beaten	1	1	1
Wholemeal flour	50 g	2 oz	½ cup
Baking powder	5 ml	1 tsp	1 tsp

1 Preheat the oven to 200°C/400°F/gas mark 6 and lightly oil a 20 cm/ 8 in flan ring.

2 To make the pastry, mix the flours in a bowl, then rub in the margarine until the mixture resembles breadcrumbs. Add enough of the water to bind to a soft dough.

3 Roll out on a lightly floured surface and use to line the flan ring. Cover with greaseproof paper and fill with baking beans, then bake blind for 7 minutes. Remove the paper and beans and return to the oven for 3 minutes. Remove from the oven.

4 Lower the oven temperature to 190°C/375°F/gas mark 5.

5 Place the pears flat-side down in the base of the pastry case.

6 Cream together the marzipan and margarine until soft and light. Beat in the eggs, then fold in the flour and baking powder. Spread evenly over the pears.

7 Return the flan to the oven and bake for 30 minutes until set and golden.

lime cheesecake

Serves 10   1.5 g fibre/270 calories per serving

	METRIC	IMPERIAL	AMERICAN
For the case:			
Soft vegetable margarine	100 g	4 oz	½ cup
Demerara sugar	50 g	2 oz	¼ cup
Clear honey	60 ml	4 tbsp	4 tbsp
Mornflake oats	225 g	8 oz	2 cups
For the filling:			
Quark	225 g	8 oz	1 cup
Greek yoghurt, strained	225 g	8 oz	1 cup
Free-range eggs, separated	2	2	2
Caster sugar	50 g	2 oz	¼ cup
Grated rind and juice of limes	2	2	2
Boiling water	30 ml	2 tbsp	2 tbsp
Powdered gelatine	15 g	½ oz	1 tbsp

A few strawberries, halved, and lime slices, to decorate

1 Preheat the oven to 180°C/350°F/gas mark 4 and lightly oil a 20 cm/ 8 in spring-clip cake tin.

2 Place the margarine, sugar and honey in a saucepan over a moderate heat and stir until dissolved. Remove from the heat and stir in the oats. Press into the base and sides of the tin.

3 Bake in the oven for 25 minutes, then remove from the oven and leave to cool.

4 Mix the quark, yoghurt, egg yolks, sugar and lime rind.

5 Mix the lime juice with the boiling water in a small bowl, then sprinkle on the gelatine and stir until dissolved. Leave to cool and begin to set, then add to the cheese mixture and leave until beginning to set.

6 Whisk the egg whites until stiff, then fold into the mixture. Pour into the prepared base and leave to set in the fridge. Garnish with strawberries and lime slices and serve within a few hours otherwise the base may go soggy.

piping chantilly cream

Makes 300 ml/½ pt/1¼ cups   0 g fibre/350 calories

	METRIC	IMPERIAL	AMERICAN
Water	60 ml	4 tbsp	4 tbsp
Gelatine	15 g	½ oz	1 tbsp
Greek yoghurt, strained	225 g	8 oz	1 cup
Free-range egg white	1	1	1

1 Place the water in a small bowl and sprinkle on the gelatine and stir. Place the bowl in a saucepan of hot water and stir until transparent. Remove the bowl from the water and leave to cool and beginning to set.

2 Stir the gelatine into the yoghurt.

3 Whisk the egg white until stiff, then fold it into the mixture and chill before use.

orange and apricot cheesecake

Serves 8   2 g fibre/200 calories per portion

	METRIC	IMPERIAL	AMERICAN
For the base:			
Wholemeal flour	100 g	4 oz	1 cup
Oat flour	50 g	2 oz	½ cup
Soft vegetable margarine	75 g	3 oz	⅓ cup
Water	45–60 ml	3–4 tbsp	3–4 tbsp
For the filling:			
Low-fat curd cheese	225 g	8 oz	1 cup
Milk	75 ml	5 tbsp	5 tbsp
Free-range eggs, separated	2	2	2
Clear honey	30 ml	2 tbsp	2 tbsp
Orange oil	3 drops	3 drops	3 drops
Grated rind of orange	1	1	1
Oat flour	25 g	1 oz	¼ cup
Free-range egg whites	2	2	2
Apricot halves	8	8	8

1 Preheat the oven to 200°C/400°F/gas mark 6 and lightly oil a 20 cm/ 8 in flan ring.

2 Place the flour in a bowl, then rub in the margarine until the mixture resembles breadcrumbs. Mix in enough of the water to mix to a soft dough.

3 Roll out the dough on a floured board and use to line the flan ring. Cover with greaseproof paper, fill with baking beans and bake blind for 10 minutes. Remove from the oven and remove the paper and beans.

4 Reduce the oven temperature to 190°C/375°F/gas mark 5.

5 Mix the curd cheese and milk to a smooth paste. Add the egg yolks, honey, orange oil, orange rind and oat flour and mix thoroughly until smooth. Whisk the egg whites until stiff, then fold them into the mixture using a metal spoon. Pour into the baked flan case.

6 Arrange the apricot halves on top of the mixture and bake in the oven for 20 minutes until set.

currant cheesecake

Serves 8   2 g fibre/320 calories per portion

	METRIC	IMPERIAL	AMERICAN
1 case from Lime Cheesecake (see page 82)			
For the filling:			
Cottage cheese	225 g	8 oz	1 cup
Thin natural yoghurt or milk	150 ml	¼ pt	⅔ cup
Soured cream	150 ml	¼ pt	⅔ cup
Currants	50 g	2 oz	½ cup
Gelatine	15 g	½ oz	1 tbsp
Boiling water	60 ml	4 tbsp	4 tbsp

1   Make and cook the case as instructed in the Lime Cheesecake recipe.

2   Rub the cottage cheese through a sieve, then stir in the yoghurt or milk and the cream until smooth. Stir in the currants.

3   Sprinkle the gelatine on to the water and stir until dissolved. Leave until beginning to set, then stir into the cheesecake mixture. Pour the mixture into the prepared case and leave in the fridge to set.

christmas pudding

Makes two 900 ml/1½ pt puddings
81.5 g fibre/155 calories per serving

	METRIC	IMPERIAL	AMERICAN
Raw cane sugar	75 g	3 oz	⅓ cup
Soft vegetable margarine	75 g	3 oz	⅓ cup
Wholemeal flour	75 g	3 oz	¾ cup
Oat flour	50 g	2 oz	½ cup
Ground ginger	5 ml	1 tsp	1 tsp
Mixed spice	5 ml	1 tsp	1 tsp
Freshly grated nutmeg	5 ml	1 tsp	1 tsp
Free-range eggs, lightly beaten	6	6	6
Unblanched almonds, finely chopped	25 g	1 oz	¼ cup
Sultanas	75 g	3 oz	½ cup
Currants	75 g	3 oz	½ cup
Raisins	50 g	2 oz	⅓ cup
Wholemeal breadcrumbs	50 g	2 oz	½ cup
Grated rind and juice of lemons	2	2	2
Brandy, rum or milk	30 ml	2 tbsp	2 tbsp

1   Lightly grease two 900 ml/1½ pt pudding basins.

2   Beat together the sugar and margarine until light and fluffy. Mix the flours and spices in a bowl, then gradually stir the flours and beaten eggs alternately into the sugar mixture. Fold in the nuts and dried fruit. Stir in the breadcrumbs. Mix in the lemon rind and juice and the brandy, rum or milk.

3   Divide the mixture between the basins, cover with a double layer of greaseproof paper and top with kitchen foil or a cloth cover. Secure with kitchen string. Place in a large saucepan and pour in boiling water to come half way up the sides of the basins. Cover and steam for 3 hours, topping up with boiling water as necessary.

4   Remove from the heat, leave to cool completely, then re-cover with clean foil or cloths. Store in a cool, dry place.

5   Steam for 1 hour before serving.

chantilly yoghurt cream

Makes 300 ml/½ pt/1¼ cups   0 g fibre/300 calories

	METRIC	IMPERIAL	AMERICAN
Free-range egg white	1	1	1
Greek yoghurt, strained	225 g	8 oz	1 cup

1 Whisk the egg white until stiff, then fold into the yoghurt. Chill before use.

2 Use instead of clotted or double cream, which has almost three times the number of calories!

rhubarb crumble

Serves 6   5.5 g fibre/200 calories per portion

	METRIC	IMPERIAL	AMERICAN
Rhubarb, sliced into 2.5 cm/ 1 in pieces	700 g	1½ lb	6 cups
Water	30 ml	2 tbsp	2 tbsp
Clear honey	30 ml	2 tsp	2 tbsp
For the topping: Wholemeal flour	75 g	3 oz	¾ cup
Mornflake oats	75 g	3 oz	¾ cup
Ground cinnamon	5 ml	1 tsp	1 tsp
Soft vegetable margarine	75 g	3 oz	⅓ cup
Stoned dates, chopped	50 g	2 oz	⅓ cup

1   Preheat the oven to 200°C/400°F/gas mark 6 and lightly oil an oven-proof dish.

2   Place the rhubarb, water and honey in a saucepan, bring to the boil, cover and simmer over a low heat for 5 minutes. Transfer to the prepared dish.

3   Mix together the flour, oats and cinnamon, then rub in the margarine until the mixture resembles breadcrumbs. Stir in the dates. Sprinkle the mixture over the rhubarb.

4   Bake in the oven for 25 minutes until crunchy and golden.

apple crumble

Serves 6   3 g fibre/235 calories per portion

	METRIC	IMPERIAL	AMERICAN
Wholemeal flour	75 g	3 oz	¾ cup
Mornflake oats	50 g	2 oz	½ cup
Sunflower seeds	15 ml	1 tbsp	1 tbsp
Desiccated coconut	15 ml	1 tbsp	1 tbsp
Soft vegetable margarine	75 g	3 oz	⅓ cup
Ground cinnamon	2.5 ml	½ tsp	½ tsp
Demerara sugar	25 g	1 oz	2 tbsp
Cooking apples, peeled, cored and thinly sliced	700 g	1½ lb	1½ lb
Juice of lemon	1	1	1
Water	45 ml	3 tbsp	3 tbsp
A few cloves			
Natural yoghurt, to serve			

1   Preheat the oven to 200°C/400°F/gas mark 6 and lightly oil a deep ovenproof dish.

2   Mix together the flour, oats, sunflower seeds and coconut, then rub in the margarine. Stir in the cinnamon and sugar.

3   Toss the apples in the lemon juice as you prepare them. Place in a saucepan with the water and cook gently for 2 minutes to soften. Turn into the prepared dish and add the cloves. Sprinkle evenly with the topping.

4   Bake in the oven for 20–25 minutes until the fruit is tender and the topping golden. Serve hot or cold with natural yoghurt.

black cherry fool

Serves 6   2 g fibre/155 calories per serving

	METRIC	IMPERIAL	AMERICAN
Black cherries, stoned	350 g	12 oz	3 cups
Greek yoghurt, strained	350 g	12 oz	1½ cups
Cold water	60 ml	4 tbsp	4 tbsp
Gelatine	15 g	½ oz	1 tbsp
Family Favourite Granola (see page 26)	225 g	8 oz	2 cups

1 Blend the cherries and yoghurt in a liquidiser to a smooth purée.

2 Place the water in a small bowl and sprinkle on the gelatine. Place the bowl in a saucepan of water over a low heat and stir until transparent. Remove from the heat and leave to cool until beginning to set.

3 Fold into the purée, pour into a container and place in the fridge to set.

4 To serve, spoon alternate layers of fool and granola into dessert glasses or sundae dishes. Serve lightly chilled.

mince pies

Makes 12   1 g fibre/125 calories per pie

	METRIC	IMPERIAL	AMERICAN
Wholemeal flour	100 g	4 oz	1 cup
Oat flour	50 g	2 oz	½ cup
Soft vegetable margarine	75 g	3 oz	¾ cup
Cold water	45–60 ml	3–4 tbsp	3–4 tbsp
Mincemeat	75 g	3 oz	¾ cup

A little milk or beaten egg, to glaze

1 Preheat the oven to 200°C/400°F/gas mark 6 and lightly oil a bun tin.

2 Mix the flours in a bowl, then rub in the margarine until the mixture resembles breadcrumbs. Blend in enough of the water to make a soft but not wet dough.

3 Roll out the dough on a lightly floured surface and cut into 12 large and 12 medium-sized rounds with pastry cutters. Press the bases gently into the bun tins.

4 Fill the cases with mincemeat, brush the edges with water and seal the tops in place. Brush the tops with a little milk or beaten egg.

5 Bake in the oven for 20–25 minutes until lightly golden.

BREADS AND TEATIME TREATS

oat bread

Makes one loaf or 10 rolls   1.5 g fibre/80 calories per roll

	METRIC	IMPERIAL	AMERICAN
Wholemeal flour	225 g	8 oz	2 cups
Oat flour	100 g	4 oz	1 cup
Fresh yeast	15 g	½ oz	1 tbsp
25 mg vitamin C tablet, crushed	1	1	1
Warm water	100 ml	¼ pt	⅔ cup
Corn oil	10 ml	2 tsp	2 tsp
Black treacle	15 ml	1 tbsp	1 tbsp
A little milk, to glaze			
Mornflake oats	15 ml	1 tbsp	1 tbsp

1 Preheat the oven to 230°C/450°F/gas mark 8 and lightly oil a 450 g/1 lb loaf tin.

2 Mix the flours in a bowl.

3 Crumble the yeast and vitamin C tablet into the water, then stir in the oil and treacle. Pour on to the flour and mix to form a dough. Turn on to a lightly floured surface and knead for 5 minutes.

4 Shape into a long 'sausage' and fold under both ends. Place in the prepared tin, cover and leave until doubled in size.

5 Glaze with the milk and scatter the oats over the top. Bake in the oven for 35 minutes until the loaf falls easily from the tin and sounds hollow when tapped on the base.

toasted teacakes

Serves 12   3 g fibre/140 calories per portion

	METRIC	IMPERIAL	AMERICAN
Wholemeal flour	350 g	12 oz	3 cups
Oat flour	100 g	4 oz	1 cup
Mixed spice	5 ml	1 tsp	1 tsp
Dried mixed fruit	75 g	3 oz	½ cup
Fresh yeast	15 g	½ oz	1 tbsp
25 mg vitamin C tablet, crushed	1	1	1
Skimmed milk, warmed	300 ml	½ pt	1¼ cups
Free-range egg, beaten with a little milk	1	1	1

No-added-sugar jam or clear honey, to serve

1 Preheat the oven to 200°C/400°F/gas mark 6 and lightly oil a baking sheet.

2 Mix the flours, spice and dried fruit in a bowl.

3 Crumble the yeast and vitamin C into the milk and leave to stand for 5 minutes.

4 Stir the yeast mixture into the flour, then add most of the egg mixture, leaving enough to glaze the tops of the teacakes. Mix to a soft dough, then turn on to a lightly floured surface and knead for 5 minutes. Return to the bowl, cover and leave to rest for 10 minutes.

5 Knead the dough again, then shape into 12 rolls and place on the baking sheet. Cover and leave to rise for about 10 minutes until doubled in size.

6 Glaze with the reserved egg, then bake in the oven for 20–25 minutes.

7 Serve split and toasted, then spread with no-added-sugar jam or a little honey.

Cook's note

Remember you can make your own oat flour by grinding some Mornflake oats or oatmeal in a food processor (see page 16).

malt loaf

Serves 10   2.5 g fibre/160 calories per slice

	METRIC	IMPERIAL	AMERICAN
Soft vegetable margarine	25 g	1 oz	2 tbsp
Black treacle	30 ml	2 tbsp	2 tbsp
Malt barley syrup or malt extract	45 ml	3 tbsp	3 tbsp
Skimmed milk	150 ml	¼ pt	⅔ cup
Wholemeal flour	175 g	6 oz	1½ cups
Oat flour	75 g	3 oz	¾ cup
Baking powder	10 ml	2 tsp	2 tsp
Raisins	100 g	4 oz	⅔ cup

1 Preheat the oven to 180°C/350°F/gas mark 4 and lightly oil a 900 g/ 2 lb loaf tin.

2 Place the margarine, treacle, malt barley syrup or malt extract and milk in a saucepan and melt together over a low heat.

3 Mix the flours and baking powder in a bowl, then stir in the raisins. Pour the liquid into the bowl and mix thoroughly. Spoon into the loaf tin and level the top.

4 Bake in the centre of the oven for 50 minutes or until a skewer inserted in the centre comes out clean. Transfer to a wire baking sheet to cool, then remove from the tin when cold.

soda bread

Makes one 450 g/1 lb loaf   3 g fibre/100 calories

	METRIC	IMPERIAL	AMERICAN
Wholemeal flour	450 g	1 lb	4 cups
Oat flour	225 g	8 oz	2 cups
Bicarbonate of soda	10 ml	2 tsp	2 tsp
Cultured buttermilk	300 ml	½ pt	1¼ cups

1 Preheat the oven to 200°C/400°F/gas mark 6 and lightly oil a baking sheet.

2 Mix the flours and bicarbonate of soda in a bowl, then stir in the buttermilk and mix to a soft dough. Work lightly until it sticks together and mould into a round. Place on the prepared baking sheet and slash the topping in the shape of an X.

3 Bake in the oven for 40–45 minutes until firm and golden, then serve warm.

date and walnut loaf

Serves 10   1.5 g fibre/260 calories per slice

	METRIC	IMPERIAL	AMERICAN
Wholemeal flour	175 g	6 oz	1½ cups
Oat flour	50 g	2 oz	½ cup
Baking powder	10 ml	2 tsp	2 tsp
Mixed spice	5 ml	1 tsp	1 tsp
Ground cinnamon	2.5 ml	½ tsp	½ tsp
Soft vegetable margarine	100 g	4 oz	½ cup
Muscovado sugar	50 g	2 oz	¼ cup
Stoned dates, chopped	75 g	3 oz	½ cup
Walnuts, chopped	75 g	3 oz	¾ cup
Free-range eggs	2	2	2
Skimmed milk	30 ml	2 tbsp	2 tbsp

1 Preheat the oven to 160°C/325°F/gas mark 3 and lightly grease a 900 g/2 lb loaf tin.

2 Mix the flours, baking powder, mixed spice and cinnamon in a bowl, then rub in the margarine until the mixture resembles fine breadcrumbs. Stir in the sugar, dates and walnuts.

3 Beat the eggs with the milk and pour on to the dry ingredients. Beat well to form a soft dough. Place in the prepared tin and smooth the top.

4 Bake in the centre of the oven for 45–55 minutes until a skewer inserted into the centre comes out clean.

Variation
Some people like to top the loaf with a little glacé icing and sprinkle with nuts.

sultana scones

Makes one large round or 12 small scones
1 g fibre/100 calories per scone

	METRIC	IMPERIAL	AMERICAN
Wholemeal flour	175 g	6 oz	1½ cups
Oat flour	50 g	2 oz	½ cup
Baking powder	5 ml	1 tsp	1 tsp
Unsalted butter or soft vegetable margarine	50 g	2 oz	¼ cup
Sultanas	50 g	2 oz	⅓ cup
Buttermilk or skimmed milk	150 ml	¼ pt	⅔ cup
A few drops of lemon juice			
A little milk, to glaze			

1 Preheat the oven to 220°C/425°F/gas mark 7 and lightly oil a baking sheet.

2 Mix the flours and baking powder in a bowl, then rub in the butter or margarine until the mixture resembles breadcrumbs. Stir in the sultanas. Make a well in the centre and gradually add the milk and lemon juice, stirring to form a soft dough.

3 Turn the dough on to a lightly floured surface and gently knead until the dough is pliable and holds its shape. Shape into a large round and place on the baking sheet. Alternatively, roll out to 2 cm/¾ in thick and cut into 12 scones with a pastry cutter. Glaze with a little milk.

4 Bake in the oven for 25 minutes for a round or 15 minutes for scones until well risen and golden.

chelsea buns

Makes 9   4 g fibre/185 calories per bun

	METRIC	IMPERIAL	AMERICAN
Wholemeal flour	225 g	8 oz	2 cups
Oat flour	100 g	4 oz	1 cup
Fresh yeast	15 g	½ oz	1 tbsp
25 mg vitamin C tablet, crushed	1	1	1
Skimmed milk, warmed	175–250 ml	6–8 fl oz	¾–1 cup
Clear honey	15 ml	1 tbsp	1 tbsp
Free-range egg, lightly beaten	1	1	1
Dried mixed fruit	100 g	4 oz	⅔ cup
Mixed peel	50 g	2 oz	⅓ cup
Mixed spice	5 ml	1 tsp	1 tsp
Unsalted butter, melted	15 g	½ oz	1 tbsp

A little milk or beaten egg, to glaze

1 Preheat the oven to 220°C/425°F/gas mark 7 and lightly oil a 20 cm/ 8 in square baking tin.

2 Mix the flours in a bowl.

3 Crumble the yeast and vitamin C tablet into the milk, then stir in the honey. Pour on to the flour with the beaten egg and mix to a soft dough. Turn on to a lightly floured surface and knead for 5 minutes. Cover and leave to rest for 15 minutes.

4 Knead lightly and roll out into a 30 x 23 cm/12 x 9 in rectangle.

5 Mix together the fruit, mixed peel and spice. Brush the dough with the melted butter, then scatter with the fruit mixture. Roll the dough into a long 'sausage' and cut into nine equal pieces. Place them cut-side up in the prepared tin, making a square with three rows of three pastries. Leave to double in size.

6 Glaze with a little milk or beaten egg and bake in the oven for 20–25 minutes until risen and firm to the touch.

cinnamon oatcakes

Makes 10   1.5 g fibre/180 calories per cake

	METRIC	IMPERIAL	AMERICAN
Soft vegetable margarine	150 g	5 oz	⅔ cup
Demerara sugar	50 g	2 oz	¼ cup
Golden syrup	90 ml	6 tbsp	6 tbsp
Mornflake oats	350 g	12 oz	3 cups
Ground cinnamon	10 ml	2 tsp	2 tsp

1 Preheat the oven to 180°C/350°F/gas mark 4 and lightly oil a Swiss roll tin.

2 Melt the margarine, sugar and syrup, then remove from the heat.

3 Stir in the oats and cinnamon and press into the prepared tin.

4 Bake in the oven for about 20 minutes until golden. Leave to cool slightly, then cut into squares.

hot cross buns
Makes 16   3 g fibre/125 calories per bun

	METRIC	IMPERIAL	AMERICAN
Wholemeal flour	350 g	12 oz	3 cups
Oat flour	75 g	3 oz	¾ cup
Ground cinnamon	5 ml	1 tsp	1 tsp
Mixed spice	5 ml	1 tsp	1 tsp
Fresh yeast	25 g	1 oz	2 tbsp
Skimmed milk	175 ml	6 fl oz	¾ cup
Free-range eggs	2	2	2
Sultanas	75 g	3 oz	½ cup
Currants	75 g	3 oz	½ cup
Mixed peel	50 g	2 oz	⅓ cup

To decorate:
Pastry trimmings
A little milk or beaten egg

	METRIC	IMPERIAL	AMERICAN
Mornflake oats	30 ml	2 tbsp	2 tbsp
Clear honey	15 ml	1 tbsp	1 tbsp

1 Preheat the oven to 220°C/425°F/gas mark 7 and lightly oil two baking sheets.

2 Mix the flours and spices in a bowl.

3 Heat the milk to blood heat, then crumble in the yeast and stir well. Leave to stand for 10 minutes, then pour into the flour, add the beaten eggs and mix to a dough. Turn on to a lightly floured surface and knead for 5 minutes. Return to the bowl, cover and leave to rest for 10 minutes.

4 Return the dough to the work surface and stretch into an oblong. Fold in the dried fruit and continue kneading to distribute it evenly. Cut the dough into 16 equal-sized pieces and form each into a roll. Place on the prepared baking sheets with space between to allow them to expand. Cover and leave to rise until doubled in size.

5 Roll out the pastry trimmings and cut into thin strips. Arrange them on the risen buns to make a cross. Glaze with milk or beaten egg and sprinkle with the oats.

6 Bake in the oven for 15 minutes until the buns sound hollow when tapped on the base.

7 Warm the honey and brush over the finished buns, then leave to cool.

no-sugar rock buns

Makes 12   2 g fibre/130 calories per bun

	METRIC	IMPERIAL	AMERICAN
Wholemeal flour	175 g	6 oz	1½ cups
Oat flour	50 g	2 oz	½ cup
Baking powder	10 ml	2 tsp	2 tsp
Mixed spice or ground cinnamon	5 ml	1 tsp	1 tsp
Unsalted butter or soft vegetable margarine	75 g	3 oz	⅓ cup
Sultanas	50 g	2 oz	⅓ cup
Currants	50 g	2 oz	⅓ cup
Grated rind of lemon	1	1	1
Milk	90 ml	6 tbsp	6 tbsp
Free-range egg	1	1	1

1 Preheat the oven to 200°C/400°F/gas mark 6 and lightly oil a bun tin.

2 Mix the flours, baking powder and spice in bowl, then rub in the butter or margarine until the mixture resembles breadcrumbs. Stir in the sultanas, currants and lemon rind.

3 Beat the milk with the egg, then add to the dry ingredients to make a moist but not sloppy consistency. Place a generous teaspoonful of mixture into each bun tin and roughen the surface with a fork.

4 Bake in the oven for 15–20 minutes until firm to the touch.

banana bread

Serves 10   0.4 g fibre/225 calories per portion

	METRIC	IMPERIAL	AMERICAN
Wholemeal flour	175 g	6 oz	1½ cups
Oat flour	100 g	4 oz	1 cup
Baking powder	5 ml	1 tsp	1 tsp
Mixed spice	2.5 ml	½ tsp	½ tsp
Unsalted butter or soft vegetable margarine	100 g	4 oz	½ cup
Muscovado sugar	50 g	2 oz	¼ cup
Free-range eggs, lightly beaten	2	2	2
Bananas, mashed	2 large	2 large	2 large
Milk	30 ml	2 tbsp	2 tbsp

1 Preheat the oven to 190°C/375°F/gas mark 5 and lightly oil a 900 g/ 2 lb loaf tin.

2 Mix the flours, baking powder and spice in a bowl.

3 In another bowl, cream together the margarine and sugar until light and fluffy. Beat in the eggs, stir in the banana, then fold in the flour. Turn into the prepared tin.

4 Bake in the oven for 35 minutes until firm to the touch.

easter muffins

Makes 18   1 g fibre/70 calories

	METRIC	IMPERIAL	AMERICAN
Wholemeal flour	100 g	4 oz	1 cup
Oat flour	50 g	2 oz	½ cup
Baking powder	10 ml	2 tsp	2 tsp
Mixed spice	2.5 ml	½ tsp	½ tsp
Ground cinnamon	2.5 ml	½ tsp	½ tsp
Soft vegetable margarine	50 g	2 oz	½ cup
Currants	50 g	2 oz	⅓ cup
Sultanas or raisins	25 g	1 oz	3 tbsp
Clear honey	15 ml	1 tbsp	1 tbsp
Skimmed milk	150 ml	¼ pt	⅔ cup
Free-range egg	1	1	1

1 Preheat the oven to 200°C/400°F/gas mark 6 and lightly oil a bun tin.

2 Mix the flours, baking powder and spices, then rub in the margarine until the mixture resembles breadcrumbs. Stir in the dried fruit.

3 Beat together the honey, milk and egg, then stir it into the dry ingredients. Spoon into the prepared tins.

4 Bake in the oven for 15–20 minutes until just firm to the touch.

mornflake fruit loaf

Serves 10   1.5 g fibre/200 calories per slice

	METRIC	IMPERIAL	AMERICAN
Mornflake oats	125 g	4½ oz	1⅛ cups
Free-range eggs	3	3	3
Caster sugar	100 g	4 oz	½ cup
Baking powder	5 ml	1 tsp	1 tsp
Stoned prunes, chopped	100 g	4 oz	⅔ cup
No-need-to-soak dried apricots	100 g	4 oz	⅔ cup
Sultanas	225 g	8 oz	1⅓ cups
Hazelnuts, chopped	100 g	4 oz	1 cup
Flaked almonds	50 g	2 oz	½ cup

1   Preheat the oven to 180°C/350°F/gas mark 4 and lightly oil a 900 g/2 lb loaf tin. Sprinkle the tin with 30 ml/2 tbsp of the oats.

2   Beat together the eggs and sugar until pale. Stir in the remaining oats and the baking powder, then the fruit and nuts. Spoon into the prepared tin and level the surface.

3   Bake in the oven for 1½ hours until a skewer inserted in the centre comes out clean. Cover with greaseproof paper at the end of cooking if the top becomes too brown.

4   This cake stores well in an airtight tin and tastes even better after a week's storage.

CAKES AND BISCUITS

christening biscuits

Makes 36 biscuits   1 g fibre/65 calories per biscuit

	METRIC	IMPERIAL	AMERICAN
Soft vegetable margarine	100 g	4 oz	½ cup
Demerara sugar	50 g	2 oz	¼ cup
Free-range eggs, separated	2	2	2
Currants	100 g	4 oz	⅔ cup
Wholemeal flour	225 g	8 oz	2 cups
Oat flour	100 g	4 oz	1 cup
Mixed spice	5 ml	1 tsp	1 tsp
Skimmed milk	150 ml	¼ pt	⅔ cup

A little egg white or milk, to glaze

1 Preheat the oven to 180°C/350°F/gas mark 4 and lightly oil two baking sheets.

2 Cream together the margarine and sugar until pale and fluffy. Add the egg yolks and stir in the currants.

3 Whisk the egg whites until stiff but not dry, then fold them into the mixture.

4 Mix the flours and spice in a bowl, then stir into the mixture with the milk and mix to a firm dough.

5 Roll out the dough on a lightly floured surface and cut out with a medium-sized pastry cutter. Place the biscuits on the baking sheets and glaze with egg white or milk.

6 Bake in the oven for 20 minutes until firm and golden.

christmas cake

Serves 20   4 g fibre/200 calories per serving

	METRIC	IMPERIAL	AMERICAN
Soft vegetable margarine	225 g	8 oz	I cup
Raw cane sugar	100 g	4 oz	½ cup
Free-range eggs, lightly beaten	4	4	4
Wholemeal flour	175 g	6 oz	1½ cups
Oat flour	50 g	2 oz	½ cup
Mixed spice	5 ml	I tsp	I tsp
Ground almonds	50 g	2 oz	½ cup
Currants	175 g	6 oz	I cup
Sultanas	175 g	6 oz	I cup
Raisins	175 g	6 oz	I cup
Mixed peel	50 g	2 oz	⅓ cup
Unblanched almonds, finely chopped	50 g	2 oz	½ cup
Stem ginger, finely diced	50 g	2 oz	½ cup
Brandy or rum	60 ml	4 tbsp	4 tbsp
Grated rind and juice of lemon	I	I	I
To decorate:			
Apricot jam	15 ml	I tsp	I tbsp
Almond paste	175 g	6 oz	6 oz
Egg white, lightly beaten	I	I	I
Almonds	100 g	4 oz	I cup
Brazil nuts	50 g	2 oz	½ cup
No-need-to-soak dried apricots	100 g	4 oz	⅔ cup

1 Preheat the oven to 160°C/325°F/gas mark 3 and lightly oil a 20 cm/ 8 in cake tin, then line it with a double layer of greaseproof paper.

2 Cream together the margarine and sugar until light and fluffy. Gradually add the eggs to the mixture alternately with the flours and spice. Stir in the fruit, brandy or rum, lemon rind and juice.

3 Spoon the mixture into the prepared tin and level the top leaving a slight indentation in the centre to allow the cake to rise. Bake in the oven for 3 hours. Leave to cool.

4 Warm the jam, then brush over the top. Roll out the almond paste and cover the top. Brush with egg white, then decorate with nuts and fruit.

honey oaties

Makes 30   0.5 g fibre/55 calories per biscuit

	METRIC	IMPERIAL	AMERICAN
Soft vegetable margarine	100 g	4 oz	½ cup
Clear honey	10 ml	2 tsp	2 tsp
Oat flour	100 g	4 oz	1 cup
Mornflake oats	150 g	5 oz	1¼ cups

1 Preheat the oven to 190°C/375°F/gas mark 5 and lightly oil two baking sheets.

2 Melt the margarine and honey over a low heat.

3 Mix together the oat flour and oats, then stir them into the melted mixture to make a paste.

4 Place heaped teaspoonfuls of the mixture on the baking sheets and flatten with the back of a fork.

5 Bake in the oven for 12 minutes until golden brown. Transfer to a wire cooling rack to cool. Store in an airtight tin.

hazelnut and carob squares

Makes 14   1 g fibre/80 calories per biscuit

	METRIC	IMPERIAL	AMERICAN
Soft vegetable margarine	50 g	2 oz	¼ cup
Muscovado sugar	50 g	2 oz	¼ cup
Free-range egg, beaten	1	1	1
Wholemeal flour	50 g	2 oz	½ cup
Oat flour	50 g	2 oz	½ cup
Carob powder	10 ml	2 tsp	2 tsp
Baking powder	5 ml	1 tsp	1 tsp
Toasted hazelnuts, chopped	50 g	2 oz	½ cup

1 Preheat the oven to 180°C/350°F/gas mark 4 and lightly oil a baking sheet.

2 Cream together the margarine and sugar until pale and fluffy. Beat in the egg. Mix the flours, carob powder and baking powder in a bowl, then fold into the mixture. Stir in the nuts and blend to a soft dough.

3 Roll out on a lightly floured surface to 5 mm/¼ in thick, cut into squares and transfer to the prepared baking sheet.

4 Bake in the oven for 20 minutes until golden and firm to the touch.

shortbread

Makes 8–10 biscuits   1 g fibre/140 calories per biscuit

	METRIC	IMPERIAL	AMERICAN
Wholemeal flour	150 g	5 oz	1¼ cups
Oat flour	25 g	1 oz	¼ cup
Light Muscovado sugar	40 g	1½ oz	2½ tbsp
Unsalted butter	100 g	4 oz	½ cup

1 Preheat the oven to 150°C/300°F/gas mark 3 and lightly oil a 20 cm/ 8 in square or round baking tin, a shortbread mould or a baking sheet.

2 Mix the flours and sugar in a bowl, then rub in the butter until the mixture resembles breadcrumbs. Lightly work to a crumbly dough.

3 Roll out the dough carefully on a lightly floured surface, then either press into the prepared tin or mould, or roll out, cut into rounds with a medium-sized pastry cutter and transfer to the baking sheet. Prick the surface with a fork and mark with a pattern if you wish.

4 Bake in the oven for 40–45 minutes. Remove from the tray and cool on a wire cooling rack. Store in an airtight tin.

Cook's note

Remember you can make your own oat flour by grinding some Mornflake oats or oatmeal in a food processor (see page 16).

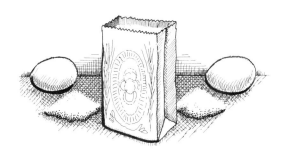

strawberry shortcakes

Makes 5   3 g fibre/350 calories per shortcake

	METRIC	IMPERIAL	AMERICAN
I quantity of Shortbread, made into rounds (see page 109)			
Strawberries, hulled	225 g	8 oz	½ lb
I quantity of Piping Chantilly Cream (see page 83)			

1 Just before serving, place half the shortbread biscuits on a flat surface.

2 Halve or slice the strawberries, or leave them whole, depending on size, and arrange them on the biscuits. Pipe the cream into the space between the strawberries and sandwich together with the remaining biscuits.

3 Offer the remaining cream in a separate bowl.

easter biscuits

Makes 24   I g fibre/75 calories per biscuit

	METRIC	IMPERIAL	AMERICAN
Soft vegetable margarine	100 g	4 oz	½ cup
Brown sugar	50 g	2 oz	¼ cup
Free-range egg, lightly beaten	I	I	I
Wholemeal flour	150 g	5 oz	I ¼ cups
Oat flour	75 g	3 oz	¾ cup
Ground cinnamon	2.5 ml	½ tsp	½ tsp
Mixed spice	2.5 ml	½ tsp	½ tsp
Currants	50 g	2 oz	⅓ cup
Milk, brandy or rum	15 ml	I tbsp	I tbsp
Mornflake oats	45 ml	3 tbsp	3 tbsp

I   Preheat the oven to 180°C/350°F/gas mark 4 and lightly oil two baking sheets.

2   Beat together the margarine and sugar until light and fluffy. Gradually add the egg. Mix the flours and spices, then fold them into the mixture with the currants. Add the milk, brandy or rum and mix to a soft dough.

3   Sprinkle the work surface with oats and a little flour and roll out the dough on top of the oats. Cut into rounds with a biscuit cutter, then transfer to the prepared sheets, oat-side up.

4   Bake in the oven for 15 minutes, then transfer to a wire tray to cool.

simnel cake

Serves 12   3 g fibre/280 calories serving

	METRIC	IMPERIAL	AMERICAN
Soft vegetable margarine	175 g	6 oz	¾ cup
Raw cane sugar	100 g	4 oz	½ cup
Clear honey	30 ml	2 tbsp	2 tbsp
Free-range eggs, lightly beaten	3	3	3
Wholemeal flour	175 g	6 oz	1½ cups
Oat flour	50 g	2 oz	½ cup
Mixed spice	10 ml	2 tsp	2 tsp
Freshly grated nutmeg	2.5 ml	½ tsp	½ tsp
Currants	50 g	2 oz	⅓ cup
Raisins	100 g	4 oz	⅔ cup
Sultanas	100 g	4 oz	⅔ cup
Raw cane sugar almond paste	225 g	8 oz	½ lb
Blanched almonds	225 g	8 oz	2 cups

1 Preheat the oven to 160°C/325°F/gas mark 3 and lightly oil and line an 18 cm/7 in cake tin.

2 Cream together the margarine, sugar and honey. Beat in the eggs, a little at a time. Mix the flours and spices in a bowl, then fold into the mixture with the fruit. Spoon half the cake mixture into the prepared tin and level the surface.

3 Roll out the almond paste to the circumference of the tin and place on top of the mixture in the tin.

4 Top with the remaining cake mixture and place 11 almonds (to represent the apostles excluding Judas) around the edge of the cake.

5 Bake for 1½–1¾ hours until a skewer inserted in the centre comes out clear. Top with double layer of greaseproof paper towards the end of cooking to prevent the cake over-browning.

coffee crunch

Makes 15   1 g fibre/90 calories per biscuit

	METRIC	IMPERIAL	AMERICAN
Wholemeal flour	100 g	4 oz	1 cup
Oat flour	50 g	2 oz	½ cup
Baking powder	5 ml	1 tsp	1 tsp
Soft vegetable margarine	50 g	2 oz	¼ cup
Fructose or raw cane sugar	50 g	2 oz	½ cup
Walnuts, finely chopped	50 g	2 oz	½ cup
Free-range egg, beaten	1	1	1
Coffee granules	10 ml	2 tsp	2 tsp
Boiling water	20 ml	4 tsp	4 tsp

1 Preheat the oven to 180°C/350°F/gas mark 4 and lightly oil a baking sheet.

2 Mix the flours and baking powder in a bowl, then rub in the margarine until the mixture resembles breadcrumbs. Stir in the fructose or sugar and the walnuts. Beat in the egg.

3 Dissolve the coffee in the boiling water, then stir into the mixture and blend all the ingredients to a firm dough.

4 Roll out the dough on a lightly floured surface and cut out with a biscuit cutter. Transfer to the prepared baking sheet.

5 Bake in the oven for 20 minutes until just firm.

fruit cake

Serves 16   3 g fibre/140 calories per slice

	METRIC	IMPERIAL	AMERICAN
Soft vegetable margarine	175 g	6 oz	¾ cup
Raw cane sugar	50 g	2 oz	¼ cup
Clear honey	30 ml	2 tbsp	2 tbsp
Free-range eggs, beaten	3	3	3
Wholemeal flour	175 g	6 oz	1½ cups
Oat flour	50 g	2 oz	½ cup
Baking powder	10 ml	2 tsp	2 tsp
Raisins	75 g	3 oz	½ cup
Currants	75 g	3 oz	½ cup
Sultanas	75 g	3 oz	½ cup
No-need-to-soak dried apricots, chopped	75 g	3 oz	½ cup
Grated rind and juice of lemon	1	1	1
Pecan nut halves	25 g	1 oz	¼ cup

1 Preheat the oven to 180°C/350°F/gas mark 4 and lightly oil and line a 20 cm/8 in cake tin.

2 Cream together the margarine, sugar and honey until light and fluffy. Gradually add the eggs with a little flour to prevent the mixture curdling.

3 Mix the flours and baking powder in a bowl, then stir in the dried fruit. Fold into the creamed mixture with the lemon rind and juice. Spoon into the prepared tin and smooth the top. Arrange the pecan nuts attractively on top.

4 Bake in the centre of the oven for 1 hour. Reduce the oven temperature to 160°C/325°F/gas mark 3 and cover the top of the cake to prevent it over-browning. Bake for a further 30 minutes or until a skewer inserted in the centre comes out clean.

sesame flapjacks
Makes 16   1.5 g fibre/160 calories per flapjack

	METRIC	IMPERIAL	AMERICAN
Soft vegetable margarine	150 g	5 oz	⅔ cup
Clear honey	60 ml	4 tbsp	4 tbsp
Demerara sugar	50 g	2 oz	¼ cup
Desiccated coconut	50 g	2 oz	½ cup
Mornflake oats	175 g	6 oz	1½ cups
Sesame seeds, toasted	50 g	2 oz	½ cup

1 Preheat the oven to 170°C/325°F/gas mark 3 and lightly oil a Swiss roll tin.

2 Melt the margarine, honey and sugar, then stir in the coconut, oats and sesame seeds. Press into the prepared tin and level the top.

3 Bake in the centre of the oven for 20 minutes until golden.

4 Remove from the heat and cut into slices, then leave in the tin until completely cold and firm before removing.

honey flapjacks

Makes 12   1.5 g fibre/180 calories per flapjack

	METRIC	IMPERIAL	AMERICAN
Soft vegetable margarine	75 g	3 oz	⅓ cup
Clear honey	150 g	5 oz	½ cup
Mornflake oats	225 g	8 oz	2 cups

1 Preheat the oven to 180°C/350°F/gas mark 4 and lightly oil a 20 cm/8 in square cake tin.

2 Melt the margarine and honey in large saucepan, then stir in the oats. Press the mixture into the prepared tin.

3 Bake in the oven for 20–25 minutes until golden brown. Mark into fingers while still hot, then leave in the tin until cold.

Variation

You can replace the honey with 45 ml/3 tbsp of golden syrup and 100 g/ 4 oz/½ cup of soft brown sugar if you prefer.

microwave flapjacks

Makes 24   1.5 g fibre/160 calories per flapjack

	METRIC	IMPERIAL	AMERICAN
Butter or margarine, softened	175 g	6 oz	¾ cup
Caster sugar	50 g	2 oz	¼ cup
Soft brown sugar	50 g	2 oz	¼ cup
Golden syrup	90 ml	6 tbsp	6 tbsp
A pinch of salt			
Mornflake oats	275 g	10 oz	2½ cups

1 Mix the butter or margarine and sugars and cook on High for 1 minute.

2 Stir in the syrup until warmed through and dissolved. Stir in the salt and oats and mix thoroughly.

3 Press into a greased 18 cm/7 in microwave dish and cook on High for 5 minutes.

4 Leave to cool slightly, then cut into squares.

crunchy carob biscuits

Makes 20   0.5 g fibre/63 calories per biscuit

	METRIC	IMPERIAL	AMERICAN
Soft vegetable margarine	100 g	4 oz	½ cup
Raw cane sugar	50 g	2 oz	¼ cup
Wholemeal flour	50 g	2 oz	½ cup
Oat flour	50 g	2 oz	½ cup
Carob powder	25 g	1 oz	2 tbsp
Coffee granules	10 ml	2 tsp	2 tsp
Boiling water	10 ml	2 tsp	2 tsp

1 Preheat the oven to 190°C/375°F/gas mark 5 and lightly oil a baking sheet.

2 Cream together the margarine and sugar until fluffy. Mix the flours and carob powder in a bowl, then stir into the creamed mixture. Dissolve the coffee in the boiling water, then add to the mixture and mix to a soft dough.

3 With floured hands, lightly shape walnut-sized pieces of dough and place on the prepared baking sheet. Press down using the back of a fork dipped in hot water to flatten slightly.

4 Bake in the oven for 12 minutes until just firm. Leave to cool on a wire rack and store in an airtight tin.

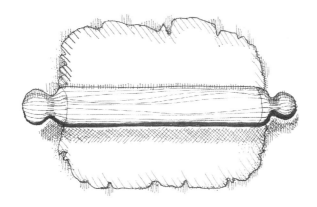

madeleines

Makes 6   3 g fibre/360 calories per madeleine

	METRIC	IMPERIAL	AMERICAN
Wholemeal flour	75 g	3 oz	¾ cup
Oat flour	50 g	2 oz	½ cup
Soft vegetable margarine	100 g	4 oz	I cup
Clear honey	30 ml	2 tbsp	2 tbsp
Vanilla essence	2 drops	2 drops	2 drops
Free-range eggs, lightly beaten	2	2	2
No-added-sugar jam, warmed	30 ml	2 tbsp	2 tbsp
Desiccated coconut	50 g	2 oz	½ cup

I   Preheat the oven to 200°C/400°F/gas mark 6 and lightly oil six dariole moulds.

2   Mix the flours in a bowl.

3   Beat together the margarine and honey together until pale and fluffy. Add the vanilla essence and gradually beat in the eggs. Fold in the flour and spoon the mixture into the prepared moulds.

4   Place the moulds on a baking sheet and bake in the centre of the oven for 25 minutes until springy to the touch. Leave to cool slightly in the tins before removing.

5   While the cakes are still warm, brush with the warm jam, then roll in desiccated coconut and leave to cool completely.

date slices

Makes 24   1.5 g fibre/125 calories per slice

	METRIC	IMPERIAL	AMERICAN
Mornflake oats	350 g	12 oz	3 cups
Soft vegetable margarine, melted	175 g	6 oz	¾ cup
Demerara sugar	30 ml	2 tbsp	2 tbsp
Ground cinnamon	5 ml	1 tsp	1 tsp
Stoned dates	225 g	8 oz	1⅓ cups
Cooking apple, cored and sliced	1 large	1 large	1 large
Water	150 ml	¼ pt	⅔ cup

1 Preheat the oven to 190°C/375°F/gas mark 5 and lightly oil a 20 cm/ 8 in square baking tin.

2 Place the oats in a bowl and stir in the melted margarine, then the sugar and cinnamon. Press half the oat mixture into the prepared tin.

3 Place the dates, apple slices and water in a saucepan, bring to the boil and simmer for about 5 minutes, stirring to a pulp.

4 Spread the date purée on top of the oats, then top with the remaining oat mixture and pat down firmly.

5 Bake in the oven for 30 minutes until golden brown. Cut into squares.

oat biscuits

Makes 14   0.5 g fibre/70 calories per biscuit

	METRIC	IMPERIAL	AMERICAN
Mornflake oats	50 g	2 oz	½ cup
Mornflake jumbo oats	50 g	2 oz	½ cup
Plain flour	100 g	4 oz	I cup
Soft vegetable margarine or butter	40 g	1½ oz	3 tbsp
Lard	40 g	1½ oz	3 tbsp
A pinch of salt			
Caster sugar	50 g	2 oz	¼ cup
Milk	30 ml	2 tbsp	2 tbsp

I Preheat the oven to 180°C/350°F/gas mark 4 and lightly oil a baking sheet.

2 Mix the oats and flour, then rub in the butter or margarine and the lard. Stir in the salt and sugar and mix to a soft dough with the milk.

3 Roll out on a lightly floured surface to about I cm/½ in thick, cut into rounds and transfer to the prepared baking sheet.

4 Bake in the oven for 15–20 minutes until golden.

piped oaties
Makes 20   0.5 g fibre/50 calories per biscuit

	METRIC	IMPERIAL	AMERICAN
Soft vegetable margarine	50 g	2 oz	½ cup
Clear honey	30 ml	2 tbsp	2 tbsp
Wholemeal flour	75 g	3 oz	¾ cup
Oat flour	50 g	2 oz	½ cup
Baking powder	5 ml	1 tsp	1 tsp
Free-range egg white, whisked	1	1	1

1 Preheat the oven to 220°C/425°F/gas mark 7 and lightly oil two baking sheets.

2 Cream together the margarine and honey until pale and fluffy. Mix the flours and baking powder in a bowl, then beat into the creamed mixture. Fold in the egg white.

3 Spoon the mixture into a piping bag with a 1 cm/½ in nozzle and pipe small circles on to the baking sheet.

4 Bake in the oven for 15 minutes until firm. Leave cool on a wire tray, then store in an airtight tin.

Cook's note
Remember you can make your own oat flour by grinding some Mornflake oats or oatmeal in a food processor (see page 16).

cinnamon crumble cake

Serves 10 slices   1 g fibre/300 calories per slice

	METRIC	IMPERIAL	AMERICAN
For the cake mixture:			
Soft vegetable margarine	100 g	4 oz	½ cup
Clear honey	30 ml	2 tbsp	2 tbsp
Free-range eggs, lightly beaten	2	2	2
Wholemeal flour	100 g	4 oz	1 cup
For the crumble mixture:			
Soft vegetable margarine	75 g	3 oz	⅓ cup
Wholemeal flour	75 g	3 oz	¾ cup
Mornflake oats	75 g	3 oz	¾ cup
Demerara sugar	50 g	2 oz	¼ cup
Ground cinnamon	5 ml	1 tsp	1 tsp

1   Preheat the oven to 190°C/375°F/gas mark 5 and lightly oil a 20 cm/ 8 in cake tin.

2   To make the cake, cream the margarine and honey until light, then beat in the eggs and fold in the flour. For the crumble, rub the margarine into the flour, then stir in the remaining ingredients.

3   Spoon half the sponge into the tin, then half the crumble mixture. Cover with the rest of the sponge and crumble.

4   Bake in the oven for 35–40 minutes until firm.

gingerbread

Serves 10   1 g fibre/240 calories per slice

	METRIC	IMPERIAL	AMERICAN
Wholemeal flour	175 g	6 oz	1½ cups
Oat flour	100 g	4 oz	1 cup
Bicarbonate of soda	5 ml	1 tsp	1 tsp
Ground ginger	10 ml	2 tsp	2 tsp
Ground cinnamon	5 ml	1 tsp	1 tsp
Soft vegetable margarine	100 g	4 oz	½ cup
Black treacle	45 ml	3 tbsp	3 tbsp
Clear honey	30 ml	2 tbsp	2 tbsp
Lemon juice	10 ml	2 tsp	2 tsp
Skimmed milk	150 ml	¼ pt	⅔ cup
Free-range eggs, lightly beaten	2	2	2

1 Preheat the oven to 160°C/325°F/gas mark 3 and lightly oil and line a 20 cm/8 in square baking tin.

2 Mix the flours, bicarbonate of soda and spices in a bowl.

3 Melt the margarine, treacle and honey over a low heat. Pour on to the flour and mix well. Add the lemon juice to the milk and add to the mixture with the eggs. Spoon into the prepared tin.

4 Bake in the centre of the oven for 50–60 minutes until firm and springy to the touch. Remove from the tin, but leave in the paper to cool.

ginger biscuits

Makes 16   0.5 g fibre/60 calories per biscuit

	METRIC	IMPERIAL	AMERICAN
Wholemeal flour	50 g	2 oz	½ cup
Oat flour	50 g	2 oz	½ cup
Baking powder	5 ml	1 tsp	1 tsp
Ground ginger	25 g	1 oz	2 tbsp
Muscovado sugar	5 ml	1 tsp	1 tsp
Soft vegetable margarine	50 g	2 oz	¼ cup
Clear honey	30 ml	2 tbsp	2 tbsp

1 Preheat the oven to 190°C/375°F/gas mark 5 and lightly oil a baking sheet.

2 Mix the flour, baking powder and ginger in a bowl.

3 Melt the sugar, margarine and honey over a low heat, then stir in the flour. Place generous teaspoonfuls on the baking sheet and press lightly.

4 Bake in the oven for 15 minutes.

staffordshire oatcakes

Makes 20   0.5g fibre/50 calories per cake

	METRIC	IMPERIAL	AMERICAN
Mornflake fine oatmeal	100 g	4 oz	1 cup
Plain white flour	100 g	4 oz	1 cup
Salt	5 ml	1 tsp	1 tsp
Fresh yeast	10 g	2 tsp	2 tsp
Sugar	5 ml	1 tsp	2 tsp
Warm milk	250 ml	8 fl oz	1 cup
Warm water	250 ml	8 fl oz	1 cup

1 Mix the oatmeal and flour in a warm bowl and stir in the salt.

2 Blend the yeast with the sugar and a little of the warm liquid and set aside in a warm place for about 10 minutes.

3 Mix the yeast into the dry ingredients with the remaining liquid to make a smooth batter. Cover with clean cloth and leave to stand in a warm place for about 1 hour.

4 Roll out on a lightly floured surface and cut into rounds. Cook on a hot griddle for about 5 minutes until browned. Alternatively you can bake them in a preheated oven at 160°C/325°F/gas mark 3 for 30 minutes until crisp.

traditional
yorkshire parkin

Serves 10   3 g fibre/160 calories per slice

	METRIC	IMPERIAL	AMERICAN
Butter or hard margarine	75 g	3 oz	⅓ cup
Skimmed milk	200 ml	7 fl oz	scant 1 cup
Black treacle	150 g	5 oz	½ cup
Soft brown sugar	150 g	5 oz	⅔ cup
Mornflake medium oatmeal	150 g	5 oz	1¼ cups
Self-raising flour	150 g	5 oz	1¼ cups
Ground ginger	10 ml	2 tsp	2 tsp
Baking powder	2.5 ml	½ tsp	½ tsp

1 Preheat the oven to 180°C/350°F/gas mark 4. Oil a 900 g/2 lb loaf tin and line it with greaseproof paper.

2 Melt the butter or margarine, milk, treacle and sugar in a large saucepan over a low heat. Stir well, then remove from the heat.

3 Stir in the dry ingredients and pour into the prepared loaf tin.

4 Bake in the oven for 20 minutes, then reduce the oven temperature to 150°C/300°F/gas mark 2 and bake for a further 35 minutes until firm.

INDEX